eBook Publishing

Part 2
Marketing and Promotion

Adrian Saunders

CONTENTS

1 INTRODUCTION

I've spent most of my forty-year career writing ad copy for a variety of newspapers, magazines and advertising agencies. This has provided me with a great deal of knowledge about advertising and marketing. A large part of that time has been spent acquiring knowledge about the most complex subject there is, human behavior and the psychology of selling products.

There are many books about the mechanics of preparing ebooks for publication. This book examines effective strategies for the marketing and promotion of ebooks rather than writing them. In it you will learn effective strategies for maximizing your book's visibility and sales with particular emphasis on the Amazon search engine aspects.

This book is based on the extensive analytical research that I have conducted over the last few months to either prove or disprove the conventional wisdom that is currently being passed off as the truth. What I found is that most of what is being taught is not verifiable and the few techniques that do produce results are both misunderstood and misapplied.

My only criterion for measuring success was whether or not a particular promotion strategy actually produced the verifiable quantitative results that were clamed for it or not. I have included more than 30 images including screenshots of all of the spreadsheets and KDP sales graphs that I used to track my results. This along with my analysis will provide the verifiable hard data for understanding how Amazon's search engine environment really functions. Once you have this knowledge you can then use it to maximize your book's visibility within that system. I simply present the reality as my testing reveled it to be.

This all started a few months ago when my friend Ray Reynolds contacted me and ask if I would help him with the marketing of a couple of Kindle ebooks that he had written. Last year he had suffered a major heart attack while undergoing minor surgery, which resulted in congestive heart failure. Because of his knowledge of the biology involved he was able to cure himself in only six months. He wrote a book about his experiences so that others might benefit from what he had learned. This book did not sell as well as he had hoped, averaging only about ten books per month. He published a second book about the most recent research in cancer treatment and prevention. This book also failed to sell averaging only six books per month.

Because of a lifetime of involvement with publishing research papers and even a couple of short academic books he was a very capable author. People who read his books left excellent reviews and having read them myself I had to agree that his books should be selling more copies than they were so I agreed to assist him with the marketing aspects of his new career as an author.

Although I owned a Kindle device and an extensive collection of e-books for it, I had never written any type of ebook let alone published one. I reasoned that it could not be much more difficult than selling any of the other multitude of products and services through any of the other types of media.

That was the beginning of what could euphemistically be referred to as a learning experience! The publication and marketing of ebooks as it turns out is an entirely different world apart from traditional sales work. Even though the psychology and philosophy of marketing anything is pretty much the same, selling ebooks on the Internet and in particular on Kindle Desktop Publishing is a world unto itself with its own special problems and traps built into it.

Since both Ray's and my work involve doing detailed research and quantitative analysis of problems during our efforts to solve them it was only logical that we would use this approach to determine why his two books were not more successful. After a few months of detailed testing the end result has been an accumulation of research data, which I am making available in this book. I hope that it will help other authors as much as it has my friend and myself.

The extensive graphs, tables and hard data from our research should be very useful for implementing your own sales strategy. While I doubt that this e-book will provide me with any significant income it has definitely been a fascinating journey of discovery on a subject, about which I previously had little knowledge. I hope you find it as interesting to read as it was for us to research and write.

The two books that we will be analyzing in detail are:

Heart failure recovery by Ray Reynolds
ASIN: B00SSJXKSE

Cancer cures by Ray Reynolds
ASIN: B011IYKJ2U

Adrian Saunders

2 HOW NOT TO MARKET YOUR EBOOK

Becoming a superstar author is most often a combination of luck and opportunity than skill and planning. Trying to achieve this nearly impossible goal will probably be a serious time waster for the average writer trying to become an author. The only way to become a successful author is to write successful books. Another thing that you need to be aware of is that because something seems logical, that does not necessarily make it true. There are many things in life that defy logic.

Another thing to understand when marketing your ebook is that fiction readers are motivated to buy books for different reasons than nonfiction readers. A fiction reader wants to escape reality; a nonfiction reader wants help dealing with reality. Most of the things that fiction writers do to attract readers will not work for nonfiction authors under even the best of circumstances. Fiction readers tend to search for new books directly in their favorite genre category rather than performing an overall search of the entire Kindle store. Nonfiction readers do the opposite by entering a very specific search phrase that is designed to only return books on that particular topic.

Writing requires a lot of time so most of the things that inhibit your success as an author will be time wasters. The two biggest ones are the belief that social media is a gateway to publishing success and that Twitter and Facebook advertising are the way to promote your book. The other misplaced belief is that you need to build and establish an author platform, which includes an enormous fan base that you will email whenever you publish a new book. Most of the authors who advise this strategy established their fan base years ago when Amazon and the Internet at large were much less competitive market places. At this point they have sufficient resources that they can outsource much of the work involved in developing, researching and writing a new book as well as maintaining their author platforms.

This system does work very well but only for established authors. It could very well be a large factor in your success five years from now when you have built up a large following that is very enthusiastic about buying your books. In the mean time you will need to work within Amazon and have a plan that will effectively promote your books until that happens.

A maximum of 35% of your email subscribers will even bother to open your emails. This is according to the companies that provide those same email list services. According to these marketing experts only 1% of that 35% will actually buy the book that you are promoting. So if you have an email list that contains 100,000 people only 35,000 of them will even look at your email before they trash it and only 350 of them will actually purchase your new book. That is a onetime sale; they will not continue to buy the same book from you month after month. The only thing that will drive continuing book sales are organic sales within Amazon itself.

Do you have any idea how long it will take you to compile a list of 100,000 opt-in email addresses? It's not going to happen in your lifetime. You will be better off spending that time writing other books and publishing them. Likewise using social media such as Facebook and Twitter to promote book sales is the biggest waste of time I have ever encountered. The marketing of any nonfiction ebook depends upon its correct presentation to the correct person who desperately needs the information that it will provide, not to the public at large. It is a very targeted process.

Everything that you need to do to promote your book on Amazon can be accomplished in about 16 hours at your computer. Anything else that you try to do as far as blogging, twitter and Facebook will be a monumental waste of your time and money. Save it for when you're famous.

If you ask the superstars of Amazon publishing who sell hundreds of thousands of copies, they probably won't be able to tell you why they are so successful. They might reference their social media accounts on Facebook or Twitter but usually the most visitors they will have is a couple thousand, most of them looking for something for free. That kind of traffic will not drive hundreds of thousands of book sales.

Most book sales are generated by the proper presentation of your book along with the proper categorization aided by the use of the correct keywords as well as being very detail oriented when it comes to setting up your book properly in Amazon itself, not through external social media advertising efforts. Amazon and kindle in particular are an environment that has been setup by its originators so that external forms of marketing have very little effect on your long term book sales internally.

A customer cannot buy what he can't find. He also will not buy your book unless he believes that it will provide the information he needs. He will not click the buy button unless you have answered all of his concerns about the efficacy of the information you're book will provide. The techniques in this book will only work if you have an excellent product to sell. The only thing that good marketing will do for a bad book is cause it to fail faster.

Author platforms

Basically this is a website where an author tries to establish sufficient traffic that it helps him sell his products. What they are trying to do through the use of social media, email lists, blog traffic and website articles is build a large enough audience that it can be used to market their book. It seems so logical on the surface but when you start digging down into the statistics it is exposed for the ineffective time waster that it is. There is only one group of authors that can successfully pull this off and those are the ones that do not need it.

Famous fiction authors have no problem at all attracting hundreds of thousands of worshipers to their social media pages or blogs. These people are attracted because the owner of that social media is famous in the first place not because the author platform itself attracts them. So basically if you're able to afford to hire people to do all of that work for you then it might be a useful tool for providing your gigantic established fan base with information about your next release thereby increasing your sales. If however you are an unknown author you won't generate sufficient traffic to make it worth the effort and expense that you put into it.

What the people who advocate the creation of author platforms don't bother to tell you is that the click through and conversion rates are so abysmally low for the emails that you send to potential customers that only one percent of them will actually purchase the book that you are promoting. There are authors on Amazon who are sufficiently well known and appreciated by their readers for producing quality books that their readers will automatically purchase any subsequent books that they write when notified by email. Unfortunately these are very rare and usually established their reputations and built their reader base early on when amazon was far less competitive.

About the only way that you can promote your book on your author website is by placing a photo of its cover in a prominent location that potential customers can click on in order to make the purchase. The number of people who see that type of advertisement and actually click on it is less than 1/2%. So if you have 10,000 unique visitors to your blog per month only 50 of them will click through to take a look at your book. Of those that examine it only 5% will actually make the purchase!

You will increase your monthly book sales by 3 books provided that all of them notice and take an interest in your book in the first place. And that's after more than a year of setting up and promoting your website. You will never be able to generate enough traffic without already being famous to drive significant book sales. In case you hadn't noticed 90% of famous authors write fiction. By the way if you're a fiction author what are you going to blog about? There's no real factual information contained in your books that you can expound upon.

J. A. Konrath (http://jakonrath.blogspot.co.uk) writes fiction and has an excellent blog that I highly recommend. The information that he provides there is not about his novels but advice to independent authors about the process of writing and publishing books and the publishing business in general. You will be far better off using the time you would normally invest in building your author platform to write more books, which is what authors do by definition. Improving the quality of your craft as well as the number of books published will do more for your sales than any amount of blogging. Unless you're already a celebrity no one will buy your book because of who you are. They will only be interested in purchasing your book because of what's inside the cover not your name.

People who follow you on a blog, Twitter or Facebook page are only interested in acquiring free information from you as well as the entertainment value that you provide. If it isn't free they won't go for it. Almost nothing that you do outside of the Kindle publication system will have any measurable effect on your sales. Best-selling books create an author platform not the other way around.

Another thing that most people do not realize is that only 20% of the US population owns a Kindle device to read e-books on. While it's true that there are kindle applications for your computer it is just not the same as curling up in a chair with a good e-book reader. Setting up and utilizing an email list service is also extremely time-consuming. Most of the services charge about $25 a month to start and that price goes up as your email list grows.

3 MARKETING AND PRICING

Whenever we attempt to promote and market a product there are a few absolute truths that we must always keep in mind when creating our ad copy whether it is written or visual.

1. Always use emotion to sell and logic to justify the sale.
When a car salesman explains all of the great safety features of a car to a prospective male customer what he is really doing is providing him with a list of logical reasons that the customer can use to justify his purchase to his family when he gets home with it. He has already made the decision to buy that particular car based on emotions rather than logic.

2. Always sell the cure not the prevention.
Even though the chance of a person having cancer at some point in their life is greater than 50% most people are not interested in any precaution they can take that might prevent this from happening. But should they already have cancer they become very proactive at finding a cure. It is always easier to convince someone to buy a cure for a problem that already exists.

Here is a list of factors that will contribute to a book's failure.

1. The subject matter is not very popular.

If you have written a book on a subject that is not popular its' sales will be very low. You can optimize your book's keywords and presentation as much as you like but if the buyers are not searching for that particular subject it will be invisible to them. This is where brick and mortar bookstores have a big advantage over ebooks.

When a potential customer walks into one he is presented with thousands of professionally produced books. It is probable that while on his way to the science fiction section he will find other books on completely different topics that interest him. He might end up buying a book on a subject that he never would have considered if he had not encountered it by accident. That is the factor that is missing from the eBook stores like Amazon. There is very little chance involved in your book being seen.

2. The main group of people who need the information do not know where to find it.

Always keep demographic issues in mind when positioning your book for maximum salability.

3. The product packaging is not sufficiently well designed to promote the product effectively.

In the case of an e-book the potential buyer can only determine the quality of the contents by viewing the ebook's cover, title, book description, author bio and by clicking on the cover image to read the first few pages. The actual product that he is buying is not accessible until after the purchase is made.

4. You have not correctly configured your keywords

If this happens to be the case your book will not be returned when the most popular search phrases for that subject are entered.

An ebook's packaging consists of the following four items in order of importance:

1. The cover.
2. The title.
3. The book description and author bio.
4. The "look inside" preview.

In the profession of copywriting beginners are continually reminded that the only purpose of the first sentence in a written ad is to force the prospective buyer to read the second sentence. The only purpose of the second sentences to force him to read the third sentence and so on until the person reaches the end and is presented with the decision to buy. Think of your ebook's "packaging" in the same way.

The purpose of the cover is to persuade the customer to read the title, the title is there to make him click the cover and go to its product page where the first sentence of the book description will catch his attention and once again cause him to read the second sentence until he is convinced that he really needs to click the cover and take a look inside. That is the sequence that will sell your book. If that chain is broken anywhere from start to finish you will lose the sale.

An important additional factor in all of this is the quantity and quality of your book's reviews. My experience is that great reviews do not help to increase your sales that much. A few bad reviews on the other hand will cause significant damage. It is more important to limit the number of 3 star or lower reviews than to generate a large number of 5 star ones. Four 4 and 5 star reviews are all that are really needed.

The successful marketing of your e-book begins with proper presentation leading to a perception of quality that ends with the delivery of exceptional content, which meets or exceeds the customer's initial perception.

The marketing of any product is an art the success of which depends greatly on the quality of the product being marketed. If you are finding it impossible to market your books the first thing you need to do is a reality-based assessment of the quality of your books as well as your marketing skills. All of the following advice assumes that your book is well written.

It is impossible to achieve success in any marketing endeavor if you do not first understand what motivates your customers to purchase your products. If you're going to be successful at writing and marketing e-books the first thing you will need to understand is what motivates readers to buy them in the first place.

More than half of all book purchases are for entertainment. People who buy and read large quantities of books are doing so because those books make them feel better either by providing them with the opportunity to live in a world more interesting than their own or by providing information that will allow them to improve their real lives significantly. The reason that self-improvement books are so successful is that they are usually both entertaining and informative as well as providing solutions for the reader's real-life problems.

The way a reader perceives a book is much more important to its salability than the actual content. Don't misunderstand me, if the content of your book is poor you will receive bad reviews and that will ultimately destroy your book's marketability. However, other than reading the preview and judging the quality of your writing by the cover art, book description and quality of the reviews it receives a potential purchaser of your book has no idea about the quality of its' contents until after he buys it.

Content quality on the other hand is the most important factor for preserving long-term market share. The thing that keeps the customer coming back to buy more of your books and recommend them to others, is the quality of their contents, and whether or not they derived enjoyment or practical advice from reading it.

Book readers can be divided into two different categories. If they are seeking escape and entertainment they will gravitate towards fiction, which is the reason that genre sells so well. The writing of this type of book requires some special skills, which require a much longer time to develop. They also depend more on natural rather than acquired abilities. So this discussion will primary focus on nonfiction writing.

The other category of potential readers are those who are seeking advice and solutions for their problems. The marketing psychology behind promoting books of this type requires you to decide whether your book is designed to move people away from a problem such as "How to stop gaining weight" or towards a solution such as "How to make money on the Internet".

Back in 2005 when e-publishing was in its infancy there was very little competition and anyone who could manage to write just about anything of passable quality was an instant success. Unfortunately this is 2015 and there are millions of authors on Amazon whose books will be competing with yours for purchaser attention. The vast majority of these books are not worth reading, especially the fiction works. They are the weeds in the Kindle e-book garden, which make it very difficult to locate the quality books.

So the first problem that you need to overcome is one of visibility. You need to make your book stand out against that background of weeds so that potential customers can find it. Despite what others may have told you this is far easier to do in theory than in practice. If you can manage to produce a successful e-book that success can then be leveraged to more quickly and effectively market other books that you write especially if their subjects happen to be related.

Pricing strategy

Quite a bit of testing has been done by myself and others on how pricing effects the sales, ranking and number of good reviews received for a book. If we increase the price of a low volume book, which has less than 25 sales per month from $2.99 to $9.99 it could very well maintain a sales rate of 15 books per month.

This would produce a gross income of $100 per month instead of the $40 per month when it was priced at $2.99. This tends to show that very specialized books that have very little competition within their niche can double their earnings when they are offered at a much higher price. We increased the prices of Ray's books from $2.99 to $3.99 with no loss of sales volume.

In order to receive a 70% royalty rate for your books you will need to price them between $2.99 and $9.99. Any price outside of this range will only provide you with the 35% royalty. Obviously Amazon is trying its best to force everyone to operate within this price range. According to their analysis your maximum profit will occur at a price of $2.99.

My experiences indicate that this is true for the average Kindle e-book. The table below provides the sale prices of three different books in three different categories showing the effect that various price points have on sales and income figures. These example books had been offered for sale for at least a month so that all of their parameters had stabilized.

Niche Size	Price/#Sales	Income	Rank	Review Increase
Low Competition	$2.99/20 per month	$40 per month	90k	.5 per month
Low Competition	$0.99/30 per month	$9 per month	50k	2 per month
Low Competition	$9.99/17 per month	$119 per month	100k	.5 per month
Mid Competition	$3.99/50 per month	$110 per month	20k	1 per month
Mid Competition	$0.99/150 per month	$50 per month	30k	1.5 per month
Mid Competition	$2.99/110 per month	$220 per month	30k	1 per month
Mid Competition	$9.99/5 per month	$35 per month	80k	1 per month
High Competition	$2.99/300 per month	$600 per month	15k	3 per month
High Competition	$0.99/600 per month	$200 per month	10k	7 per month
High Competition	$9.99/1 per month	$7 per month	35k	1 per month

A low competition book is one that is located in a category where there are few competitors. It is on a subject about which less than 200 books have been written the best of which have sales of 20 to 40 books per month. Books about specific medical conditions would fall into this category. There is a relatively low demand for them but the people who are looking for them are very motivated to find a solution for their particular problem. The demand for this type of book changes very little relative to its pricing. Overpricing a book in this particular category will probably not damage its popularity so long as the quality is good. There are large numbers of Kindle owners who only purchase $.99 books this is what accounts for the increase in purchases when you price your book at $.99 but these are more from impulse than necessity.

A mid competition book is one that is located in a category with about 700 competing books the best of which are selling about 200 copies a month. Overpricing a book in this particular category can result in bad reviews as well as damage to your sales to the point that it may take a long time to recover when you reduce the price back down to the lower level. Comparing the price of similar books to yours within this category to determine what yours should be is the correct course of action. $2.99 will probably produce the greatest amount of income per month. Many readers in the mid and high competition range will not pay more than $2.99 for a book the same as some readers will not pay more than $.99 for one.

A high competition book is one that is located in a category where there are a maximum number of competitors. This category would have 2,000-6,000 books listed. The bestsellers will sell 600 or more copies per month. Excessively high prices in this market can cause even more damage to your reputation and the salability of your book long term even after the price is reduced because of bad reviews that you might receive. What you need to do here is to survey other books with comparable content and page length to determine what the average price is and price yours accordingly. An initial price of $2.99 is probably the best place to begin.

Price matching is the way to go for both mid and high competition books. Determine what the average price of the competition is and then price accordingly. Otherwise if in doubt use the $2.99 price point.

The $.99 price point generates a greater number of purchases and therefore more reviews. A book that is purchased for $.99 is expected by the reader to deliver a relatively small amount of information. When he downloads a truly well written and formatted book that normally would be priced at $3.99 he feels that he got such a great deal that he's more willing to leave a review for that book. The greater sales that are generated will also increase your ranking within the Kindle system. Obviously if your book is already selling well and has a decent ranking there is absolutely no reason to discount it to $.99 and suffer the loss of income as well as the pollution of your also bought list with books about inappropriate subjects.

If you have just published your book and it is already generating sales of more than one copy per day at a price of $2.99 then you're doing very well and should wait for a month and see what happens. Always remember that a nonfiction book is a need-based item. If a person needs the information in that book they will pay whatever is necessary to get it. This is what makes books in smaller niches potentially more profitable. But at the same time you need to balance volume of sales against the potentially higher price that you can charge. With fewer competitors it's much easier to position yourself and your book as the authority on that subject and therefore the most desirable one to purchase regardless of its price.

You can always change the category that your book lives in at any time that you want, so if you have consistently poor sales perhaps you need to examine other categories that might provide better results. Whenever a book that has been listed on KDP for awhile is moved to a new category the Kindle search engine treats it as though it was a newly uploaded book with all of the promotional perks that a new book has for the first month.

Occasionally updating your older books with additional data and information and then marking it as a revision when you re-upload it lets potential readers know that you're maintaining it. So whenever your book starts to slip in sales ranking adding 10 - 20% content, re-uploading and then changing its categories slightly could revitalize your sales. There are services that you can subscribe to such as hugeorange.com that will promote your book on a continuing basis thereby helping to maximize and maintain its profitability.

The only way to find out if you have what it takes to survive as an author is to write and publish that first book. Learn from your mistakes and publish a second one that's even better. Try different genres. In this way you will learn what makes the publishing market work and what readers like. You will also find that your perspective about writing as well as your development as an author will mature and change along the way.

Persuading Amazon to market your ebook

Amazon will do a great deal of the marketing for you. Some of the reasons that this works so efficiently are as follows.

1. Amazon is the largest bookseller in the world and sells more than a half billion Kindle ebooks per year. The Kindle store accounts for 70% of ebook sales worldwide.

2. Amazon also has one of the world's easiest to use purchase systems. If someone wants to buy a Kindle e-book they only need to click a button and five minutes later they are reading the book.

All of this makes Amazon the world's largest search engine dedicated to the purchase and shipment of merchandise. If you give them half a chance they will market your book for you and target very precisely the people who are most interested in purchasing it. In order to initiate this process there are a number of things that you must do and do very well to get your book to the tipping point where Amazon will consider it worth promoting.

Getting the most out of Amazon's free marketing services

Kindle e-book purchases account for 70% of world e-book sales. Since Amazon profits from each e-book sale they are very interested in promoting buyer interest through a system of marketing that has been developed over a ten-year period. When their automated promotion system starts noticing your book it will begin promoting it to potential purchasers, which of course will increase your book sales, which in turn causes Amazons search engine to promote it with ever greater enthusiasm.

The more successful your book is the more Amazon will promote it and the more Amazon promotes it the more successful it will be. All of this produces a synergistic circle of marketing that produces ever-increasing book sales for you. Obviously you want to do everything in your power to help this automated system to help you! We will be learning how to implement the following key marketing strategies in the subsequent chapters of this book.

1. Carefully selecting your keyword phrases. We will examine this in the next chapter.
2. Selecting the two categories in which your book will be most visible and competitive.
3. Creating a title, which contains as many keywords as possible.
4. Adding a subtitle, which is descriptive of your book's contents and contains additional keyword phrases.
5. Designing an eye-catching cover that will generate interest.
6. Crafting a book description, which will create further interest and persuade potential buyers to read the "look inside" preview.

Everything that we do during the marketing phase of our e-book is designed to prove to Amazon that our book is worthy of their promotional efforts. As was mentioned earlier Amazon's search engine updates all of their bestseller lists hourly. This "recency bias" means that your book's ranking within the search engine will start dropping almost immediately if it is not selling. Here is a list of the things that will provide your book with the best possibility of rising to the top of its bestseller category listing and remaining there.

Do a proper initial $0.99 launch as presented in chapter ten to generate paid ranking for your book. Make sure that it is located in at least one category where it will always be in the top 10%. This will make it infinitely more visible to Amazon's search engine and encourage it to recommend your book to other potential customers who are doing searches. This will lead to higher sales and increased visibility within the Amazon marketplace. This cycle feeds upon itself and produces enough organic sales that your book will remain in an elevated position for a long time to come. Although your book's popularity will drop over time, if you have established it sufficiently well in the beginning it will be slow and your book will generate steady income for a year or more. When its sales finally drop too low you can always do a revision or addition of content and re-promote it.

The "also bought" listings

One of the most important results of a high ranking that generates sales within a category is that your book will start appearing in Amazon's "Also bought" listings. These are the rows of thumbnail book cover images that appear at the bottom of any book page that you go to. These show other books that the purchasers of the book that is currently being displayed have bought.

This is one of the most important aspects of Amazon's marketing system. If your book is popular enough and highly ranked enough it will appear in this row of titles and will be seen by more customers thereby further promoting your book and increasing your sales. If a customer is interested in one book about a particular subject he will also be interested in buying additional books about that same topic. It will take about two months for a low volume book like the ones we are examining to start making these connections to other similar books. Do not run more free or .99 promotions for your book after this occurs or you will destroy all of these good connections to other similar books.

If your new book initially sells well within a short period of time it will also show up in the "Hot new releases" section within its category listing. If it has a consistently high review rating there's a good probability that it will show up in the top rated section of its category also. These can also result in your book being featured on the bestsellers list. Amazon also continually emails its customers with book suggestions based upon their previous purchases.

Recording your successes with screenshots

Whenever your book reaches any milestone you should record that fact by making a screenshot. Make sure that your screenshot includes your entire computer monitor window so that the date in the information bar is visible.

Book tracking tools

1. KDP reports

In the menu above your bookshelf's homepage you can click on "Reports" to check the daily sales for any of your books.

2. Author Central

Your author Central page lets you track your book's Kindle ranking over longer periods of time so that you can examine statistical data for your book sales and ranking from the beginning of its launch. You can also track your create space paperback edition sales here as well. You can also check your author ranking, which is based on overall book sales both historical and current.

E-book tracker website

This is a free Internet service that allows you to track not only your own book sales but those of other authors as well. tracker.kindlenationdaily.com

I hope that at this point you understand how important it is to position your book as high as possible within the Amazon e-book ranking system. Proper positioning of your book within that system is the only way that you will achieve success and position yourself as an authority about that particular subject. This in turn will maximize your book sales and lead to ever-greater success as an author as you continue to publish other works whose success will be fueled by the success of your previous books.

4 SEARCH PHRASES AND KEYWORDS

Keywords and Search Phrases

These are the words that people type into search engines to locate needed information. In the case of the Kindle search engine people type in a search word or phrase that best describes what book topic they are looking for.

Keywords have "tails"

To be more precise they have short, medium or long tails. This actually refers to the length of the keyword phrase. A keyword phrase that only has a single word would be considered "short tailed", one with two or three words would be considered "medium tailed" and one with four words or more would be referred to as a "long tailed" keyword. Usually a short keyword phrase is much less specific than medium or long tailed phrases and will return a greater number of results.

How search engines parse your keywords

When you enter a search phrase such as "The difference between a cat and a dog" into Amazon's search bar the first thing that it does is remove all of the articles so that it is left with "difference between cat dog" it will probably then eliminate the word "between" as being irrelevant to the meaning. So it is left with "difference cat dog". It will also turn any plural nouns into their singular form.

Once the search engine has eliminated all extraneous vocabulary it will parse its way through a look-up table that contains (in order of importance) the title, subtitle, book description and keywords of every book that it sells.

If a customer enters the search phrase "cancer cures" the search engine will find and list any books that contain both of those words in its title before any others. Next it will list any books that have those two words in the subtitle. Then books that only have one of those words in their title and of course then it would apply the same rule to the subtitle. It would then perform the same matches with any words in the description and then the keywords that were entered when the book was uploaded.

If there are two books tied for a position the search engine will use other factors such as sales rank and number of positive reviews to break the tie. Normally the sales rank is no taken into consideration only the prevalence of the customer's search phrase keywords in the appropriate places.

This is an oversimplification of the process as there are many other factors that are involved in the ranking of the books that are returned in search results but this will give you some idea of the importance of correctly selecting your keywords and then designing your title around them so that your book ends up on the first page of those results where the potential buyer will be sure to see it.

Selecting appropriate keywords and phrases

Just to the left of the Amazon search bar there is a small gray rectangle where you can select the specific area of the store that you want to search. Click on it and select Kindle store from the drop-down menu. You can now enter the primary keyword that describes the subject of your book into the search bar. When you enter that word a drop-down menu will appear, which contains the most popular two word phrases that people use when searching for that primary topic in descending order of popularity. After writing down any search phrases that appear add a space after the word you typed in.

Be sure to make a list of these popular search phrases the first time you enter a word because once you type in a phrase and hit return to test it Kindle's search engine will store it and the next time that you enter the primary word it will list any phrases that you typed in yourself. This will contaminate the list with your own entries rather than showing only the ones previously entered by other shoppers.

One problem that can occur when a very large number of people are searching for a specific book title is that you can end up with a suggested search phrase that is based specifically on that book's title. This will be sorted out in the next step when we test the various phrases that are returned to determine their suitability as keyword search phrases.

If you enter the word "cancer" followed by a space the following search suggestions will appear:

Cancer
Cancer memoirs
Cancer books
Cancer diet
Cancer stories
Cancer Ward
Cancer cure

Obviously if your book is about cancer its title will probably contain that word. The remaining two word phrases listed above are in descending order by frequency of use. So those are obvious keyword phrases to use when you are asked to enter your seven keywords during the book file upload process. Obviously you should disregard any search phrases that are not appropriate for the subject mater contained in your book.

Notice that the number one search phrase is "cancer memoirs". Emotions are what sell any product not logic or thirst for knowledge. For the most part people are looking for emotional stimulation. Keep that in mind when you are writing any type of book. If there is a very emotional personal angle that you can include in your story it will increase your sales by more than 100%.

Not only is Amazon telling you the exact phrases that people use to find your type of book but they also list them in descending order of popularity. If you can manage to work one of those short phrases into your title or subtitle it will boost your sales considerably. If that is not possible be sure to use any appropriate ones for your keywords entry as well as in your book description when uploading your manuscript to KDP.

The next step in the process would be to type in the keyword cancer followed by a space and the letter "a" this will return another dropdown list of the most popular search phrases that start with the word cancer and have a second word that starts with "a". Add any of those that are appropriate to your list and continue on through the alphabet doing the same thing for each letter. When you reach Z put an "a" in front of the keyword as this will produce the same type of results only with the suggested words being in front of the main keyword instead of after.

The next step in the process is to type each of your keyword phrases into the Kindle search bar and examine what type of books each of them brings up. If those books are consistently similar to yours and are selling well then you're probably on the right track as far as keyword selection is concerned. The general public never sees the keywords that you enter when uploading your e-book file. They are only used by the Kindle search engine to help customers locate the type of book that they are searching for.

Most of you are probably wondering how you will manage to enter 20 or 30 keyword phrases when KDP only allows you seven. In actual fact KDP limits you to six comas, which will be used to separate seven keyword phrases. These phrases can be as long as you want them to be. Each one of the seven keyword phrases can be 50 words in length if you want. I'm sure there must be some upper limit to the total number of words that you can enter but I haven't found it yet. This is very different from CreateSpace where you are only allowed 5 keywords with a maximum of 25 characters each.

You need to understand that the search engine does not parse your keywords for their combined meaning. It is only trying to find individual keywords that match the individual words that are contained in the customer's search phrase. So the rules for entering your keyword phrases are as follows:

1.Do not repeat any keywords. Multiple entries of the same word are not necessary. So if you're listing 20 different types of cancer you only need to enter the word cancer once.

2. Each phrase can have as many words in it as you want. So although you're limited to a total of seven keyword phrases you can actually enter as many words between the commas as you want. So far as the search engine is concerned you could place all of the adjectives in one keyword phrase then all of the adverbs in another followed by all of the nouns and verbs in their own individual phrase. Only the groups of words need to be separated by commas. The search engine is not intelligent and does not understand the meaning of the customers search phrase. It is only looking for the individual words. If it discovers those words somewhere in your title, subtitle, Book description or keywords it will tell the customer about your book. The category you place your book into is irrelevant to this parsing process UNLESS the customer deliberately selects a specific category to search in. That does not happen very often. Probably 95% of all searches are of the entire kindle store.

Below are tables of all of the search phrases for all three books and below them is the list of keywords that we uploaded to KDP when we published the books. This should give you a really good idea of how it's done. In one of the following chapters are screenshots of the keyword spreadsheets so that you can see how effective this method is for positioning your book on the first or second page of the search results and how its' position varies over time and with sales.

Cancer Cures book keyword phrases

Keyword = Phrase typed into Amazon search bar

#Books Returned = Total number of books returned by search.

Book Position = Position of Cancer Cures book on list of books.
A book position number of 16 or less positions a book on the first page of the books returned, which is where you want it to be. A position of 32 or less places it on the second page, which is still viable. If its position is greater than 32 it is essentially invisible to shoppers.

Notice how the phrase "Cancer Cures" places the book in position three on the first page of the search results out of 624 books. That is the title of the book and shows how much emphasis the search engine places on search words being in the title. The reason "Natural Cancer Treatments" puts the book in position two is that there are fewer books returned and the word "Treatment" is in the subtitle as well as the book description. We will fine-tune the title in the next chapter to exponentially improve these results. It is very much a two-part process.

Keyword (search phrase)	#Books Returned	Book Position
Cancer	6,400	75
Cancer Cures	624	3
Natural Cancer Cures	144	2
Natural Cancer Treatments	96	8
Cancer Stories	1,000	31
Cancer Treatments	1,600	22
Alternative Cancer Treatments	272	6
Alternative Cancer Prevention	80	5
Cancer Prevention	38	6
Breast Cancer Cures	144	5
Breast Cancer Treatment	144	31
Breast Cancer Prevention	144	18
Breast Cancer	1,900	63
Colon Cancer	288	13
Colorectal Cancer	176	8
Leukemia	544	9
Lung Cancer	450	36
Prostate Cancer	688	56
Melanoma	320	15
Skin Cancer	336	18
Chemotherapy	1,470	20
Radiation	2,150	17

Actual Keywords entered during upload to KDP

Cancer brain lung leukemia colon skin melanoma pancreatic prostate carcinoma breast colorectal, angiogenesis anticancer radiation therapy natural alternative holistic treatments, prevention medicine medical, alternative, treatment, cure chemotherapy, memoirs diet books stories nutrition

Where the comas are placed is irrelevant as long as there are less than six. There are 32 words and 5 comas. I could add another 100 keywords if I thought it would do any good.

Heart Failure Book Keyword Phrases
Keyword = Phrase typed into Amazon search bar
#Books Returned = Total number of books returned by search.
Book Position = Position of Heart Failure book on list of books.
A book position number of 16 or less positions a book on the first page of books returned, which is where you want it to be.

The reason that this book sells so much better than the Cancer Cures book is that it has been listed in Kindle five months longer and its' three main search phrases are used in its' title.

Keyword	#Books Returned	Cancer Book position
CHF	32	1
Heart Failure	600	10
Congestive Heart Failure	275	1
Heart Health	3,400	106
Heart Disease	2,700	48
Heart Attack	500	20

Actual Keywords entered during upload to KDP
chf, heart failure, congestive heart failure, coronary heart disease, heart health, heart disease, heart attack

It took no more than 3 days for the search engine to get this "pecking order" sorted out. There is at most a 2-day latency period before the search engine sorts out new keywords and promotes your book according to them.

Once you have determined precisely which phrases and keywords are most often used by people who are searching for books similar to yours you can specifically inform the Kindle e-book search engine that it should refer your book to people who are searching for those particular words or phrases. You can also incorporate them into both your title and subtitle as well. Any of the keywords that you use in your title and subtitle need not be repeated when you enter your seven keyword phrases as the search engine always gives words within the title and subtitle preference when ranking possible choices for a customer.

A recap of how Amazon searches for books

1. By book title

Amazon's search engine will first try to find the closest matches amongst all of the book titles and subtitles that are listed in Kindle. This is why it's so important that your title and subtitle be as close a match with the subject material of your book as possible. If it is possible to use any of the keywords that you develop in the previous steps it will help your book's search ranking. This is the reason that e-book subtitles are so long. The authors stuff as many keywords into them as is possible. You should never compromise the quality of your title by stuffing it with keywords that are awkward or seem out of place.

2. By keyword

The seven-keyword phrases you entered when you upload your book. When you actually upload your book there will be a text box where you can enter the seven-keyword phrases that you think are most appropriate for your book. These will be the second most important source of information about your book content that the search engine can use to determine if your book's subject matches the search phrase that the customer entered.

3. By book description

The book description that you enter on your books landing page is the other important reference for the search engine. It is 4000 characters long or about 800 words and it is quite easy to include a large number of keywords and keyword phrases that will help increase your books ranking within a customers search results.

Now that you have your list of keyword phrases that prospective buyers will use when searching for your book it is time to optimize everything so that Amazon's search engine will rank your book in the top 10% of whatever category you place it in. Whenever a perspective buyer types one of your phrases into Kindle's search bar its search engine starts looking for books about that particular subject matter.

The primary search is for titles or subtitles that contain the same words as the search phrase that was typed in. Next to be parsed are the book descriptions. The third is the keywords that you will enter into your books data page during its' upload to KDP.

Notice that the word "category" has not been used in connection with a books search ranking. That is because it is completely irrelevant! Think of categories as old shoeboxes that are being used to store memorabilia. Some of them might contain what the box says on the cover but others might not. Do not read beyond this chapter until you completely understand the implications of that!

Using Google Adword search to determine your keywords

Don't bother! In my opinion it has a rather steep learning curve and often returns misleading information. People are doing very specific searches for book titles and topics in Kindle. Not for information in general as they do in Google. The results you obtain through Google keywords will be much less accurate than those you obtain from Kindle. Most often people searching for a book will not use Google at all because they know exactly where to go for their book downloads and that is Amazon.

Adrian Saunders

5 CATEGORY SELECTION

Choosing your book categories

This is one of the most important things to get right when publishing your e-book. Amazon allows you to select which two categories within their file hierarchy your books belong in. This is the one thing that will most effect the success of your book but perhaps not in the way you think.

The first step in choosing the best two categories for your book is to do a search for other books on that topic and then click on them and see which categories they are using in their product details section. If possible you should try and list your book in two different e-book categories. As shown in the two examples below you can list a book on cardiovascular health under both Cardiology and Cardiovascular Diseases.

Kindle Store > Kindle eBooks > Medical eBooks > Internal Medicine > Cardiology

Kindle Store > Kindle eBooks > Medical eBooks > Diseases > Cardiovascular

The first one is the most competitive and is where a buyer might search by category to find that type of book. The other is one of the least competitive categories in Kindle Store with only 10 books in it. It is impossible for the Heart Failure book not to be in the top 10 books for that category and receive all of the special treatment that the search engine gives books in the top 10% of each category.

There are two different category listings that are used on Amazon. The general one that is used by Amazon customers to search for books is unique to Amazon. The second, which is the one that you will be using in KDP to categorize your book is based on the standard BISAC book cataloging list that is used throughout the book industry. Unfortunately they differ slightly from one another so it can initially be slightly confusing. If when you are in the process of categorizing your book you can't find a direct match in KDP for the categories in Amazon, which will actually be searched by the potential customers. The best thing that you can do is come as close as you can. Using the Cardiovascular category mentioned above as an example I had to email the technicians at Amazon and ask them to do it for me, which they accomplished within 24 hours.

Choosing a competitive category

Throughout this process keep in mind that once you select your two categories you're not stuck there permanently and can change them at any time in the future. If your book sales do not seem to be doing as well as you think they should you can try changing categories to see if it makes any difference. If it doesn't you can always reverse the process and change back to your original ones. It usually takes about 48 hours for the new category to appear on your book's product page.

Also remember that you should not play around with your category listings until you are sure that your keyword search phrases are working properly and that your book is starting to appear on page 1 or two when your search engine keyword phrases are typed into the search bar. If you use the correct keyword phrases it will probably take the search engine less than a week to sort everything out and bring your book up to page one or two of the search results for those phrases. So wait about a week before you make any category changes.

You must now do the necessary research to determine how easy it will be for your book to rank in the top ten books of your chosen category. Initially it is best to put it in a category that is not as competitive as the others so that fewer sales will be required to maintain its' position in the top ten. This will greatly increase the visibility of your book and the frequency with which Amazon recommends it to potential customers who are searching for that type of book. Your book's greater visibility will in turn generate more sales, which will of course help to keep it in the top ten.

To rank their books Amazon uses what is called a moving average which is updated every couple of hours. This means that if you have no sales within a given period of time, usually a few hours, your book will drop in ranking. It usually takes about seven days of zero sales for it to drop from the number one position in a category to the 100th position.

Usually the shorter the search phrase the greater the number of books it returns. When we enter one of our search phrases we can check at the bottom of the book list that it produces and determine exactly how many pages of 16 books are listed. The number of books per page varies according to your browser magnification settings so count them prior to assuming there are 16.

For the previous cancer keyword phrases they are as follows:

Keyword (search phrase)	#Books Returned	Book Position
Cancer	6,400	75
Cancer Cures	624	3
Natural Cancer Cures	144	2
Natural Cancer Treatments	96	8
Cancer Stories	1,000	31
Cancer Treatments	1,600	22
Alternative Cancer Treatments	272	6
Alternative Cancer Prevention	80	5
Cancer Prevention	38	6
Breast Cancer cures	144	5
Breast Cancer treatment	144	31
Breast Cancer prevention	144	18
Breast Cancer	1,900	63
Colon Cancer	288	13
Colorectal Cancer	176	8
Leukemia	544	9
Lung Cancer	450	36
Prostate Cancer	688	56
Melanoma	320	15
Skin Cancer	336	18
Chemo		
Chemotherapy	1,470	20
Radiation	2,150	17

The ranking of books presented by keyword search are not ranked by their ABSR numbers but solely according to their keywords. 1,000,000 ABSR ranked books are often ahead of Ray's in searches even though his book's ABSR numbers are 60k to 200k.

If you were to place your book in the general cancer category no one would ever wade through the 5 pages of 16 books each and find it. If on the other hand the subject matter of your book deals in some way with alternative cancer treatment you can list it in that category and only have 272 books competing with it for reader attention. It will now be in position 6 on page one of the search results and everyone will see it. Your book may be ten times better than any of the others but no one will ever know if they are not able to locate it, and unless it appears on the first or second page of search results it will probably never be found.

Because of the fact that any person who enters the search word "cancer" will be presented with this same drop-down menu of suggestions they are very likely to click on one of those recommended keyword search phrases rather than think up and enter their own.

A book with an "Amazon best sellers rank" of 10,000 overall is selling about fifteen copies per day and one with an ABSR of 30,000 is selling approximately ten. In each of the categories that are appropriate for your book you should select the 10th book in the top 100 paid list and check its ABSR number. If it is 30,000 than your book will need to sell 10 copies a day to remain in the top 10 of that category.

Below is a table of the approximate ABSR rankings (June 2015)

ABSR	Daily Sales
1	6400
100	1000
500	131
1,000	113
2,000	90
3,000	70
4,000	52
5,000	34
7,000	22
10,000	15
15,000	14
20,000	13
25,000	11
30,000	10
40,000	8
50,000	5
70,000	3
90,000	2
100,000	1

To determine which category would be best for your book enter your keyword phrases one at a time into the Kindle search bar and hit return. You're looking for ones that result in a booklist with the following approximate statistics.

About 100-200 books total results (6-12 pages)
No more than 1,000 results (62 pages)
At least one very popular book on page 1
At least one less popular book on page 1
A lot of books doing poorly (on all pages)

A position on page one that your book is capable of taking over

You want to make sure that the "sort by" menu located at the top right hand corner of the window is set to relevance (this is the default).

The other possible choices are:
Featured
Price low to high
Price high to low
Average customer review
Publication date.

These are very useful for determining other book parameters when doing other types of research.

Once you know which books are associated with the search phrases that best describe your book you can then click on the thumbnail of each book and scroll down to its "product details" section. The part that you're interested in is at the very bottom and will look something like this.

Amazon Best Sellers Rank: #24,950 Paid in Kindle Store

#8 in Kindle Store > Kindle eBooks > Medical eBooks > Internal Medicine > Oncology > Cancer
#8 in Kindle Store > Kindle eBooks > Health, Fitness & Dieting > Diseases & Physical Ailments > Cancer > General

#31 in Books > Health, Fitness & Dieting > Diseases & Physical Ailments > Cancer

You can now click on the last subcategory word (Dark Blue) in each of the category indexes. This will take you to the top 100-bestseller list for that category. You can then check the ABSR for the 10th most popular book in that category to see if yours would have a chance at selling the same number of copies as it and displacing it.

By examining this data you can determine that particular book's ABSR as well as the two categories that the author has chosen for it. If that book has the same type of content as yours and is performing well for its author then those categories will probably work for your book as well. Now check the remainder of the top 10 books in that category to see if yours would be competitive. I use KDSPY for all of the research as it saves hours of work. You can check it out at http://www.kdspy.com It is currently $47 and well worth it.

Once you get a feel for the main categories that best fit your book you can make note of the number of books in those categories (they are in parenthesis next to the category name) and then click on the main category and try to find a subcategory that has the fewest books in it but still matches some aspect of your books content. Here are the categories I placed the books we are studying in.

Cancer Cures book
Amazon Best Sellers Rank: #202,402 Paid in Kindle Store

#8 in Kindle Store > Kindle eBooks > Medical eBooks > Internal Medicine > Oncology > Chemotherapy

#91 in Kindle Store > Kindle eBooks > Health, Fitness & Dieting > Diseases & Physical Ailments > Cancer > General

#91 in Kindle Store > Kindle eBooks > Medical eBooks > Internal Medicine > Oncology > Cancer

The first thing to make note of is the ABSR, which is 202,000. The Main category rank (cancer) is 91 and the book is about to drop off the 100 best sellers list for that category. But in the second category chemotherapy it's still ranking number eight.

This means that Amazon's search engine considers it to be a very popular book and is currently promoting it as a bestseller in spite of its' very low ABSR. This is one of the best examples of category selection that you will find and it's what you need to do for your book as well.

The most profitable nonfiction book categories

Here are some examples of the more profitable subcategories in nonfiction. The 42 most popular nonfiction categories with average number of books sold per day by each of the top twenty books in those categories are listed below.

Find one of these you will enjoy writing books in and you will prosper as a nonfiction author. This information is from http://k-lytics.com. You should go there and watch their free promotional video. It will confirm what I am telling you in this book and provide additional information that will be very useful to you.

Nonfiction-Self-Help		250
Nonfiction-Biographies & Memoirs		250
Self-Help-Motivational		190
Nonfiction History		175
Nonfiction-Health, Fitness & Dieting		175
Religion & Spirituality-Christian Books & Bibles	170	
Nonfiction-Politics & Social Sciences		120
Biographies & Memoirs-Memoirs		115
History-Americas		95
History-United States		95
Children's eBooks-Growing Up & Facts of Life	90	
Nonfiction-Business & Investing		85
Self-Help-Personal Transformation		80
History-Military		80

Biographies & Memoirs-Women		80
Biographies & Memoirs-Professionals & Academics	75	
Health, Fitness & Dieting-Counseling & Psychology	70	
Nonfiction-Science		65
Politics & Social Sciences-Social Sciences		65
Religion & Spirituality-Spirituality		60
Business & Money-Management & Leadership	60	
Biographies & Memoirs-Leaders & Notable People	60	
Literature & Fiction-Mythology & Folk Tales		58
Biographies & Memoirs-Arts & Literature		55
History-World		50
Children's eBooks-Fairy Tales, Folk Tales & Myths	45	
Business & Money-Business Life		45
Nonfiction-Sports		45
Politics & Social Sciences-Politics & Government	43	
Biographies & Memoirs-True Crime		43
Nonfiction-Parenting & Relationships		40
Health, Fitness & Dieting-Relationships		40
Nonfiction-Cooking, Food & Wine		38
Business & Money-Entrepreneurship & Small Business 38		
Religion & Spirituality-New Age		38
Health, Fitness & Dieting-Diets & Weight Loss	35	
Nonfiction-Travel		35
Nonfiction-Crafts, Hobbies & Home		35
Nonfiction-Children's Nonfiction		35
Business & Money-Skills		34
History-Europe		30
Health, Fitness & Dieting-Nutrition		30

If you have a book in the top 20% of any of these fiction categories it will be making you $2,000-4,000 per day. Now you know why every category on Kindle is flooded with romance and erotica novels.

Literature & Fiction-Women's Fiction

Mystery, Thriller & Suspense-Suspense

Mystery, Thriller & Suspense-Suspense

Literature & Fiction-Contemporary Fiction

Mystery, Thriller & Suspense-Mystery

Romance-Contemporary

Literature & Fiction-Genre Fiction

Literature & Fiction-Literary Fiction

Romance-Romantic Comedy

Romance-New Adult & College

Adrian Saunders

6 CREATING AN EFFECTIVE TITLE

The most important information on this subject is at the end of this chapter. It will make your book as much as ten times more visible during customer keyword searches.

Never start a book title with "Introduction to…" or "How to…" It will be buried under all of the other books that start the same way.

Research indicates that consumers first look at a physical book's:

Title
Cover
Back cover
Table of contents
First few paragraphs of the book's content
Price

If the author is well known that can be an important factor as well. If the author is very well known and popular it can be the most important factor. If the author is unknown it is not a negative factor but simply a nonfactor. Notice that price is the last consideration.
No one has ever said looks like a great book. If only it was one dollar cheaper I'd buy it. As long as the book is perceived to deliver value equal to its price that price will be paid.

The title

The title of the book is multifunctional. It is the second opportunity to influence a potential buyers opinion of your book. Once the potential customer has been hooked by your cover art the second thing that will produce continued interest in your book will be its title. There are two basic concepts that need to be understood about title construction.

1. Your title must inform the reader of the subject matter of your book and do so in a way that stimulates the reader's curiosity and convinces him that your book will provide either information or entertainment in the case of fiction that he so desperately needs.

2. Your book's title should contain as many keywords as possible without being awkward since the Kindle search engine will examine it and the subtitle as well to determine the subject matter of your book. A popular search word that is included in your title or subtitle will cause your book to rank higher in customer book searches than any other factor. Baking bread might be a good title for a how to book on making bread.

You could further distinguish your book by subtitling it "Baking Bread the Artisan Way" perhaps you could do a series of books on baking such as:

Series Title of all books.
Baking Artisan Breads

Series Subtitles
"Baking sourdough breads"
"Baking Italian breads"
"How to bake four and twenty blackbirds in a pie"

You need to match the title of your book as much as possible with the search words that the reader will be entering to find that type of book.

The category you place your book in is almost irrelevant. Categories are the kindle equivalent of an old shoebox that you store things in under the bed. The label on the lid might say Nike Shoes but inside are old baseball cards. Properly conceived and entered search phrases are what will make your book visible to buyers in the kindle store no mater what category it is parked in.

This will cause the Kindle search engine to rank your book much higher in that category when it looks for books to recommend to buyers based on relevancy. Fiction is an exception to this rule because readers of fiction usually search in fiction categories for new interesting books in very specific genres of novels that they like to read.

The subtitle
This is your third chance to hook the customer.

1. Your book's subtitle is your third opportunity to make a positive impression on a potential customer. It should expand upon the title and provide additional information that will convince the potential buyer that this is the book that will solve his problem.

2. The subtitle should contain a couple of strategic keywords as the Kindle search engine gives added weight to information contained within the title and subtitle when recommending your book to customers.

Obviously the title is extremely important in determining the sales volume of a physical book. The same is equally true for e-books. You want yours to be as persuasive and compelling as possible.

The problem of course is thinking up a great title for your book. Don't feel like you're alone, the think tanks at the traditional publishing houses hate it when they have to come up with the title for a new book as well. The criteria that they use for determining a title's suitability for a new book are as follows.

Does it:
1. Make a promise
2. Create intrigue
3. Identify a need
4. Simply state the book's content.

Some necessary characteristics of a title are as follows

Is the title easy to remember a week later?

Does the title create curiosity and make you want to know more about the book?

Does the title offer value? Is there an implied promise to the reader of benefit?

Would the reader feel embarrassed if someone saw them reading a book with that title? Titles that people consider offensive or dated can reduce book sales.

Does it use power words that compel the reader to pick it up?

These are the basic factors that will elevate your book title from boring, to successful. If you're the type of person who prefers a more formulaic approach then here's the standard formula for generating an Internet headline.

Number + adjective + topic noun + item + benefit = viral title.
Here are some examples that were generated by typing the verb
"fart" into the title generator at:

http://tweakyourbiz.com/tools/title-generator/index.php.

6 Critical Skills To Fart Remarkably Well
12 Horrible Mistakes To Avoid When You Fart
8 Irreplaceable Tips To Fart Less And Deliver More
7 Reasons Why You Can't Fart Without Social Media
Fart Once, Fart Twice: 8 Reasons Why You Shouldn't Fart Thrice

Another important issue is whether the title is brandable or not. A
good example of this concept for nonfiction books would be Tim
Ferris's bestseller "The four hour workweek", which allowed him to
be identified with his series of "Four hour books".

Quite often just changing one or two words in a title can make a
tremendous difference in sales volume.

The squash book 1,500 copies
The zucchini cookbook 300,000 copies

Patent Medicine and Public Health 3,000
The Truth About Patent Medicine 10,000

The Sonnets of a Portrait Painter 500
The Love Sonnets of an Artist 6,000

The Mystery of the Iron Mask 11,000
The Mystery of the Man in the Iron Mask 30,000

Poems of Evolution 2,000

When You Were a Tadpole and I Was a Fish 7,000

Instead of beating your head against a wall trying to shake something loose there are several websites that you can go to that have title creation engines that can be used to generate hundreds of title examples from your input. They are meant to be used by bloggers to develop titles for their blog posts but they work equally well for generating titles for books.

These generators utilize standard power words and phrases to produce attention-grabbing titles. If this type of headline produces greater click through rates for bloggers it should perform just as well for an e-book title. They generate title copy using phrasing that has been tried and tested by some of the best marketers in the world.

Here are some websites that provide this free service:

http://tweakyourbiz.com/tools/title-generator/index.php

http://www.contentforest.com/ideator

https://www.portent.com/tools/title-maker

http://www.hubspot.com/blog-topic-generator

http://www.contentrow.com/tools/link-bait-title-generator

Here's a title-rating tool that will tell you what they think of your book title's buyer appeal. This one is excellent!

http://www.aminstitute.com/headline/

We changed the title of Ray's heart book from "Congestive Heart Failure Recovery" with the subtitle "From Complete Failure to Complete Recovery" to "Heart Failure" with the subtitle "From complete Heart Failure to Heart Health"

The number after each search phrase is the total number of pages of 16 books each returned by the search. The numbers in the other two columns indicate the position of the book in the search results. A "1" indicates that it was the first book a "10" the tenth book etc.

Search Phrase	Before Change	After Change
CHF2	1	1
Heart Failure38	10	1
Congestive Heart Failure17	1	1
Heart Health216	122	13
Heart Disease170	69	27
Heart Attack31	21	5

We changed the title of his cancer book from "Cancer Cures" with the subtitle "A Synergistic Approach to Cancer Prevention and Treatment" to "Cancer" with the subtitle "Cures, a Synergistic Approach to Cancer Prevention and Treatment"

Search Phrase	Before Change	After Change
Cancer400	221	21
Cancer Cures39	11	4
Cancer Stories63	35	4
Natural Cancer Cures9	10	5
Natural Cancer Treatment6	11	9
Cancer Treatment99	23	10
Alternative Cancer Treatment	15	2
Alternative Cancer Prevention5	4	9
Cancer Prevention38	23	6
Breast Cancer Cures9	9	10
Breast Cancer Prevention9	27	12
Breast Cancer Treatment9	42	3
Breast Cancer120	105	29
Colon Cancer18	16	11
Colorectal Cancer11	17	1
Lung Cancer28	43	13
Prostate Cancer43	75	13
Leukemia34	22	37

I would call that a significant improvement! I am not certain as to why there should be such a difference between "Cancer Cures" and "Cancer". Obviously much experimentation is needed whenever you create a title so that you discover anomalies such as this. Even the search phrase "cancer cures" gives better results when the title is just "Cancer" than when it is "Cancer Cures". That is not logical! This only seems to work when the most common search phrase used is a single word such as "cancer".

If searching for books on "heart failure" titling them just "heart" would probably not work. However naming a book "Knitting" or "Baking" then a subtitle that expands upon it probably would be very effective. This is why you need to publish the Kindle version of your book before your CreateSpace version so that you can perfect the title before committing yourself to a title in CreateSpace that can never be changed.

It may be because everyone who searches for books on cancer only enter "Cancer" instead of more detailed search phrases so the search engine has decided that cancer is the one to treat preferentially. This shows that when we are searching for books on a subject we need to be very diligent about using a variety of detailed search phrases to avoid missing appropriate books that will not be found with more general search phrases.

When your title is only one word you need to make sure that other potential search words are located elsewhere in the subtitle, keywords and description. I will continue my research in this area and upload that new information in the first revision of this book in about two months, which you can then download free of charge because you have already purchased it. I will also be including the statistics for this book and others that I research. Check back every couple of months for higher revision numbers than what you currently have.

After uploading this book to KDP and doing the first round of testing I found that none of the obvious search phrases found it so I changed the title from "Reality based Kindle Publishing" to just "Kindle Publishing". Immediately after the change was reviewed and approved the search phrase "kindle publishing" returned it in the number four position on the first page of results out of 400 pages of books. I will continue optimizing all of its' parameters and include that information in the first revision to this book in a month or so.

7 COVER DESIGN

A couple of freelance sites were you can find plenty of higher priced e-book cover designers are: elance.com and 99designs.com.

The later is an interesting site where you tell them how much you're willing to spend for your cover and a group of designers will offer you their interpretations of what you want. This allows you to pick and choose amongst them to find the best possible option for the amount of money you're willing to pay. You want to make certain that any designer you use understands the basic parameters that you are looking for.

Do not try to control the actual design itself but you should give sufficient input so that the designer knows in which direction you want to go without micromanaging him. Make certain that he understand that whatever design he presents to you will ultimately be viewed as an image no larger than 2 inches in height. This will greatly affect how they design the cover since a lot of detail will not be as visible as it would if the cover were 6 x 9 inches in size.

When a reader views your book cover it will probably be about the size of a postage stamp. That doesn't offer much wiggle room for proper presentation. You want to make certain the title is clearly legible. Your subtitle probably will not be readable without eyestrain but as long as the title and the overall cover design provide enough incentive for the person to click on it that's all that's needed.

The information that your book's cover must convey to potential readers is more about general concept rather than the actual content. A reader's response to a particular cover that is well designed is more instinctual and emotional than cognitive. Leave the plot line to the book description. Your cover needs to contain elements that will grab your potential readers attention on an emotional and visceral rather than intellectual level.

The first part of your cover research should involve examining all of the covers of the top 100 best sellers in your category. This will give you a very good indication of what types of cover art your potential readers are used to seeing. Now have something designed that is exactly the same but entirely different.

You then need to arrive at an overall concept that will work. No amount of font size and type adjustment or image changes will salvage a poorly conceived cover. A good way to test whether or not your cover conveys the correct concept is to try it out on your friends and acquaintances and see if they are able to guess what type of book the cover is for.

A special issue with e-book covers is they spend most of their life as a thumbnail image. This limits what you can do so far as detail is concerned. You should concentrate on the message that the image as a whole conveys rather than the details. Once you've arrived at what you think is an ideal cover you should display it alongside the other thumbnails in the top 100's best-sellers for that category and see if it is both similar in concept but at the same time stands out from the rest of them.

If you create your own e-book cover I can guarantee that you it will have an idiot for a graphic designer! I don't care how good you really are or how good you think you are. Hire someone who is qualified to do the design work. This is not expensive, difficult nor time consuming. Here are the two covers that Ray designed himself for his e-books. It probably cost him close to $100 worth of time to design each of these turkeys!

Here are some covers that we had designed for $10 each on fiverr.com

These first 2 are by vikiana.

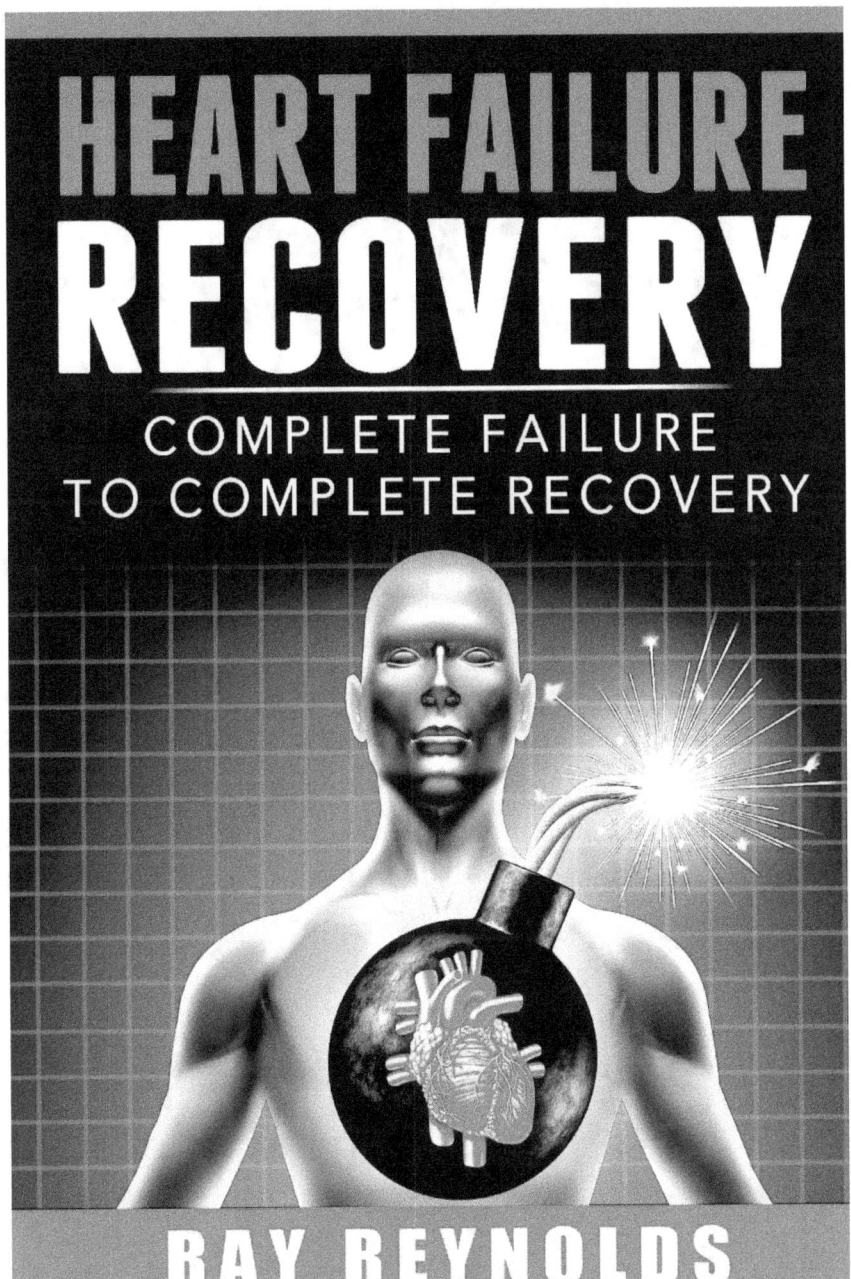

CANCER CURES,

THE LATEST RESEARCH

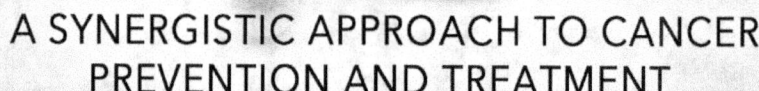

A SYNERGISTIC APPROACH TO CANCER PREVENTION AND TREATMENT

RAY REYNOLDS

Here are the same cover themes as developed by alerrandre another fiverr.com cover designer.

CANCER CURES
THE LATEST RESEARCH

A
Synergistic
Approach
to Cancer
Prevention
and Treatment

RAY REYNOLDS

There is more to designing an e-book cover than copying and pasting images and text. Like any other art it requires both natural talent and years of practice to develop an instinct for what will work and what won't.

1. Go to fiver.com and type "Kindle cover design" into the search bar.
2. Select "high rating" above the thumbnail images for the various cover designers.
3. Move your cursor over the thumbnail images to reveal the names of the designers.
4. Both vikiana and alerrandre will be among the top 10 designers listed.

The cost of designing the cover itself is five dollars. You should also pay the additional five dollars so that the designer can purchase the rights to the image he uses on your cover. This insures that you have the legal right to use that image however you desire. When you download the finished cover the original of that image will be included with it separately so that you will have access to it in the future if you need it to make changes. You then click the pay button and you will be redirected to your PayPal account where you can either use your PayPal balance or a credit card connected to it to pay for your cover.

As soon as you have paid you will immediately be redirected to the cover designer's dialogue window where you will fill in any information that the designer will require to produce your cover. This includes the following:

1. The book title
2. The subtitle
3. The author's name
4. Any additional text that will appear on the cover.
5. If it is a fiction book you might want to include your book description. If it is a nonfiction work you should probably include the table of contents along with the description as well. So that the designer will have an idea of what the book is about.

Since you are usually limited to 1200 characters in the dialog window it might be easier to put all of your information into a Notepad or TextEdit file and attach it to your message. Click send and then about three days later the designer will notify you that it's time to review your cover. You will then have the opportunity to review it prior to download and request any changes that you think are necessary. You then click download and the file will be downloaded to your computer.

Once you've tested the cover on the Kindle version of your book and are absolutely certain that you will not change the title or subtitle in the future you can then order a create space version of the same cover from the same designer for about $20.

By the way, I provided no image or graphic design information, only the general topic and table of contents for the books along with the title, author and any other text that needed to be placed on the covers. Both designers found their own images and came up with their cover designs with no additional input from me. I did assign the same projects to four other top rated cover designers but these two produced the most consistent quality.

This whole process is completely painless and takes less than 10 minutes. After you're done you can continue writing your book instead of wasting your time producing a cover that will cause your book to be a failure!

If it really bothers you to get a great e-book cover for only $10 then you might want to try:
http://archangelink.com/book-covers/ $129

For $129 they will not only provide you with a cover but also assist you with the sale of your first hundred books.

8 WRITING EFFECTIVE AD COPY

Copywriting is a form of creativity that produces financially functional works of art. A great piece of ad copy is like a crouched tiger in a forest full of cuddly pandas. Its' whole reason for existence is to spring everything of importance on you in a compact manner, that, like a bucket of ice water in the face, requires no footnotes or explanations. Comparing literature to great ad copy is like comparing a star to a singularity. The one provides warmth and comfort; the other sucks you in to its event horizon where you are consumed.

The production of those literary singularities is what this chapter is about. Creativity and inspiration are the building blocks of all original thought. When these two intellectual conspirators are combined with knowledge of the world at large, they produce outside the box thinking that leads to inspired results. While it is impossible to teach the creative part in this short chapter I should be able to get you up to speed on the basics, which will enable you to write very acceptable book descriptions. The mechanics of copywriting is a very linear process involving the generation and refining of prose resembling nothing so much as an assembly line for manufacturing goods.

It has repeatedly been proven that any eight-year-old child of average intelligence given less than an hour's instruction on the rules of copywriting is fully capable of writing very effective ad copy on subjects that are of interest to them. Adults sadly seem to require long periods of study and tedious textbooks to accomplish the same. Practical examples of actual book descriptions will be presented in the next chapter.

Nobody wants to buy your nonfiction book!

Sorry to be the bearer of bad news but there is absolutely no one in the world who wants to buy your book. Normally people do not buy a hammer because they are collectors who consider it a work of art that they are going to frame and hang on a wall. They buy that hammer for the very specific purpose of pounding a nail into a piece of wood and the hammer was designed to fulfill that need perfectly. This is the main difference between a fiction novel and a nonfiction advice book. Fiction authors cater to a reader's wants whereas a nonfiction writer supplies a reader's need for information.

When someone makes the decision to purchase a "how to book" they are doing so because it is perceived to fulfill a need that they have. Women do not buy sheep fat that has been dyed red and placed in tubes to smear on their faces. They buy lipstick to make themselves more beautiful. People do not want books; they want the solutions that those books can provide for them.

Whenever you write a book description you need to keep that in mind and make certain that you inform the potential customers about the specific benefits that ownership of your book will provide for them.

The difference between a benefit and a feature.

Since features are physical, books do not usually have them so the information on the next couple of pages is presented here for reference and will usually only be applicable to physical items you may want to sell.

Most often when people try to list the benefits of an item they are actually listing its' features. If what you're describing begins with:

It does…
It is…
It has…
We are…
Then you are describing your products features such as:

Our microwave has fan assisted convection heating
We provide one-click financial reports
It is fully mobile compatible
Our images are copyright free
We are a local supplier
Our new all-terrain bike has 20% lower gearing

The features of your product are what provide the benefits to the customer. Letting the customer know what the benefits are is what will sell your product to them not listing its features. There is a very simple process for determining what those benefits are. All you need to do is attach the phrase "Which means…." to the end of the sentence that describes a feature and then complete the sentence. That second part of the sentence will describe how that particular feature benefits the customer. Let's apply this concept to the six previous statements describing features.

Our microwave has fan-assisted convection heating, which means faster more even cooking.

We provide one-click financial reports, which means you get immediate information and prepared statements for your accountant.

It is fully mobile compatible, which means you can access your application from your cell phone.

They are copyright free, which means you are free to use them commercially.

We are a local supplier, which means we understand the specific needs of local retailers.

Our new all-terrain bike has 20% lower gearing, which means you can climb steeper hills.

Advantages

An advantage in advertising is something that you can offer your customers that none of your competitors are providing. This in essence gives you an "advantage" over your competitors.

An example that shows all three concepts discussed so far, as they would apply to a book might be:

Feature
This book contains all the information you will need to solve your problem.

Benefit
You will only need to buy one book instead of several, paying one low price for all of the information.

Advantage

No other book offers such complete coverage of the subject at such a low price.

How to write a quality book description.

Writing ad copy that convinces a prospective customer to purchase a particular product always goes through a very linear process, which is very easily described and utilized for generating your book description. In advertising it is often said that the sole purpose of the title is to force the reader to read the subtitle and that the only purpose of the subtitle is to make that person read the first sentence of the ad copy.

While this is to some extent an exaggeration what they're trying to point out is that if the prospective customer does not read the entire ad copy then it is obvious that he will not arrive at the "Buy Button" and make the purchase. Properly written ad copy must be an unbreakable chain that leads as directly and effectively as possible from the title to the purchase of the item. This is true whether the ad copy is written to sell a bicycle or an ebook.

People in general and especially the younger demographics no longer read anything sequentially from start to finish they are skimmers and scanners who skip through an article visually looking for something that catches their attention. If whatever attracted their attention fails to maintain their interest then within a couple of seconds they will start scanning again until they discover something else that is worthy of their attention.

The purpose of properly written ad copy is to short-circuit this skimming process forcing the person to focus on the beginning of your copy, which will then lead them linearly through your presentation resulting in a sale. Because Amazon's Kindle store is a visually rich environment this linear presentation of your book will be even more image dependent.

This means that your book cover is the most important element of your ad copy. If it is not properly designed and presented the prospective customer will never have the opportunity to read the remainder of your presentation and be convinced to make the purchase. Your ebook "sales ad" should consist of the following linear flow of elements.

1. Get their attention with a great cover.
The first step is to capture the reader's attention with striking cover art. This is why it's so necessary to develop an exceptionally attractive cover for your e-book as well as an attention grabbing title. Once you've gotten their attention it will only last for a few seconds before they satisfy their curiosity and move on to reading something else. This is the most critical moment for selling your book. The sale depends completely on the ability of your cover and title to convince the person to click on it so that he can read the book description. If your cover and title are not 100% perfect that will not happen.

2. Use the title and subtitle to convince them that the book will solve their problem.
Use a short and descriptive title to inform them of your books subject mater followed by a subtitle that provides additional information.

3. Use your book description to increase their interest making them read the first part of your book creating a desire to buy it.
You're Book description needs to begin with an interesting title that catches a person's attention and should be an h3 size header. Below it should be a smaller subtitle that logically results from that title and

expands upon its' subject matter.

4. List the benefits that reading your book will provide.
Present a bullet-list of things that the prospective buyer will learn from your book.

5. Additional author and book information.
Provide additional interesting information about the book and author that will help to establish his credentials and credibility.

6. Recommend the purchase of the book.
Believe it or not you have to end the book description with a recommendation that the reader buy the book. Research has proven that this increases sales by 25%.

Techniques for improving your basic ad copy
There is a great deal of difference between spoken and written English. Spoken English is both very direct and simple, which is precisely the tone of voice that we need for selling. Unfortunately because of our experiences with high school and elementary school English courses whenever we sit down to write we immediately switch to written English mode, which is completely useless as a sales tool.

For a good example of truly great ad copy let's take a look at a sales brochure from the Apple computer company. In it they use the word iPhone 81 times. They use Apple 26 times but they use the pronouns you and your more than 100 times! The reason for this is that they are talking as though they are addressing a single person not a room full of potential customers. You would not say " Xerox is grateful for your continuing support as a customer!" but rather "We are grateful for your continuing support as a customer!" A company is a thing and it's impossible for it to have any sort of feeling.

Ad copy will almost always use short simple sentences with short simple words. Simple ideas expressed simply. Quite often these short sentences consist of only one word. "How do they feel? Comfortable!" " Who can benefit? Everyone!" You can get away with things in ad copy that would never be approved by your high school English teacher like beginning a sentence with "And". "Here at gingerbread house we bake the lightest cakes ever. And the most delicious!". "It's the best deal on the market. And it comes with a 100% money back guarantee."

Contractions such as we're, you'll, they'll and shouldn't are also permitted as well. This reinforces the customer's perception that you are speaking directly to each one of them rather than to a room full of potential victims.

Seeding curiosity
How do you lead the reader from the end of one paragraph to the start of the next? One method is to generate curiosity using paragraph tags similar to the ones that follow!

> But there's more.
> So read on.
> But I didn't stop there.
> Let me explain.
> Now here comes the good part.
> And here's why.
> And it only got better

If you end your paragraph with one of these or a similar teaser it will force the reader to continue reading the next paragraph in your sales copy.

The emotional aspects of copywriting

So far you have learned that every element contained within a written advertisement is there for the sole purpose of persuading the prospect to read the first sentence. The next step was to make sure that the lead-in sentence to your proposal was simple and riveting forcing him to read the second and third sentences and so forth. The creation of a proper environment in which to make your presentation as well as the necessity of creating a resonance and harmony between you and the prospective buyer is also needed. This encourages him to believe in you and agree with your statements.

You need to implement the slippery slide concept by creating an effortless path flowing through your ad copy that will carry the reader inevitably to the end of your presentation.

At this point you have all of the major tools that are needed to write an effective book description. Now let's explore the nuances that will make your success even more certain. Thus far we have not mentioned anything about the actual selling of the product or the proper way to go about enumerating its benefits or features.

Use emotion to sell but logic to justify the purchase.
Changing a single word within your copy can increase sales by as much as 20% simply because of the emotional impact that it conveys. Many words that mean the same thing have entirely different feelings. Violin/Fiddle or Repair/Fix are words that mean the same thing but elicit entirely different emotional responses.

People who buy luxury automobiles such as BMW or Mercedes when asked why they did it always cite technical features that those cars contain, which they found very attractive. While that may be true, 80% of the real reason for making that purchase was emotional and subjective rather than logical. The safety and technical features, though important are only used to justify the purchase, which was actually based on emotion. Emotion is the major reason that fiction books sell so much better than nonfiction.

When writing ad copy you first get your reader to slip into an emotional mindset as a result of the verbal and visual environment you have created. Many advertisements for products end with the statement "If not 100% satisfied return your item within 30 days for a prompt and courteous refund." How can a refund be courteous? That statement is not logical but appeals to emotion. It indicates to the customer that the company he is about to do business with is both respectful and understanding. This ability to sense the intrinsic difference in word emotion is something that has to develop over time and from testing different words in the same ad copy.

Rational and emotional motivators.

The rational
Improving profits
Reducing costs
Better efficiency
Dependability
Easier and more cost-effective maintenance
Utility
Security
Health and safety

The emotional
Pride
Fear
Comfort
Not wanting to look foolish
Envy
Laziness

Approval
Conformity

Calls to action (CTAs)

To quote the Bible "Ask and ye shall receive." the copywriter version of that is "If you don't ask you won't get."

The sole purpose of any ad copy is to persuade someone to do something. This can include such things as:

1. Opting in on your email list
2. Buying your book.
3. Signing up for a service
4. Downloading something
5. Contacting you for more information
6. Leaving a review for your book

If your ad copy does not succeed in generating one of those responses then it is not ad copy it is simply a broadcast of information. All ad copy is meant to generate some type of response on the part of the reader. In copywriting these types of requests are referred to as "Calls to action". There are two purposes for using them.

1. It moves a potential customer further along in the sales process.
2. It is a measure of the effectiveness of our copywriting.

Number 2 is very important and is one of the best ways to measure the effectiveness of a book description. By making minor changes to it every month or so we can determine what wording works best by monitoring long term sales.

Good and bad CTA practices

According to current e-marketing research verbs generate far more participation than do adjectives, adverbs and nouns for eliciting responses to CTA's. Bold, confident, commanding verbs such as: Buy, register, subscribe, donate and download have been proven to increase the response rate for calls to action. Instead of the standard "click here" button a far better approach is to include more detailed information about what type of benefits the person who clicks on that button will receive.

Such as:

Read more on the blog

Download your personal copy

Take a free tour

Claim your exclusive…

Time fencing, the art of adding urgency to your CTA

This price is good only for the first 100 orders

Offer expires today

First 100 lucky people only

Immediate download

People really like things that are immediate as well as downloads. That last one delivers on both counts. Just add the word free between them and you have an instant winner!

Eliminating risk

Click here for your no obligation 30-day free trial

Remember you have a 100% money back guarantee

You've nothing to lose

Removing barriers

One of the great joys of electronic marketing is that everything happens at the speed of computer rather than snail mail. Amazon has perfected that system to its ultimate form with their "one click shopping system".

9 YOUR BOOK DESCRIPTION

In the previous chapter you learned how to use Basic copy writing skills to improve the quality of your book description. In this chapter we'll take a look at the practical application of these skills by creating book descriptions for the two books we are studying.

The book description that you upload during your publishing process will also be used by the Kindle search engine to decide whether to recommend your book to a potential customer. Keywords that you deliberately include in your description should appear to be a natural part of the narrative and not contrived. Your book description needs to be a work of art and marketing strategy as well as a simple statement of the book's purpose.

This is a great opportunity to provide the potential customer with detailed information about your book's content and purpose. It should be composed of shorter paragraphs to make it easier for your customer to read and assimilate. Placing a list of bullet points in between paragraphs when appropriate is one way to accomplish this. You want to keep everything as simple and straightforward as possible.

Your book description can contain a maximum of 4000 letters or about 800 words. If you're going to incorporate Amazon HTML code into your description that will probably use up about 200 characters leaving you 3,800 characters for your actual description.

The decision to purchase a book is based upon its' reviews, the title, the cover, and book description. Now that you have optimized your keyword phrases and placed your book in the proper categories you will have a relatively large volume of potential buyers examining your book to determine whether or not it will solve their particular problem. Unfortunately if you have done an inadequate job of presentation the buyers will lose interest in your title and move on to examine one of your competitor's books instead.

When it comes to marketing any kind of product packaging is far more important than the actual contents so far as making a sale is concerned. Quality content is what guarantees you sales volume, repeat customers and brand loyalty. Your book can have the best content ever created but it will not sell unless the customer is sufficiently interested in the cover and title to open the book and read what's inside. All successful books will have the following:

1. An attractive interesting cover.
2. A title and subtitle that convince the buyer that this is the book he needs to solve his problem.
3. A few four and five star reviews but more importantly no 3 star or lower.
4. A great book description.

When a potential buyer examines your book description he will be trying to determine the following:

1. What is this book about?
2. Will it solve my problem?
3. Will it deliver what the title and cover say it will?

4. Is enough information provided for me to make a decision?
5. Do I like the way the book is described?
6. Does the description inspire me?
7. Does the author have a good writing style?

If you write a book description that addresses all of these concerns properly you're almost guaranteed a sale. You should put as much work into writing your 800 word book description as you did writing the actual book. As an unknown author the only hope you have of being successful is a proper presentation of your book. The first thing you need to do when you write a book description is "Stop thinking like an author and start thinking like a copywriter!"

Begin by researching as many of the descriptions written by your successful competitors who have authored similar books. This is particularly true if you can find a book similar to yours that was originally published by a traditional publishing company. I can guarantee you that its' book description was written by a professional copywriter who was paid very well for his efforts. His work should serve as an excellent example of what you are attempting to achieve.

It would also be worth your time to read a good book that explains the process of copywriting. A little education will put you way out ahead of the other independent authors who are competing with you. Your book description must successfully convey the following information to the potential buyer:

1. What problem will this book solve?
2. How will it provide the solution?
3. What will happen if the reader doesn't solve their problem?
4. What benefit will the buyer receive from this book?
5. What new information will this book provide?
6. What does this book promise to do for the reader?
7. Is the author sufficiently qualified to write about this subject?

8. Has the author completely described the problem the buyer is attempting to solve?

9. Describe the obstacles that will prevent your potential readers from achieving their objectives.

10. What kinds of mistakes will this book correct or prevent?

Don't overcomplicate your description, stick to the main theme. You should write the book description in present tense, second person using you and your as though you are talking directly to the reader. Use powerful descriptive vocabulary to describe your book.
Such as:
Four proven strategies to…
A guide to…
A proven blueprint for…

Each sentence of your description from the start to the finish should compel the buyer to read the following sentence. Use as few adjectives and adverbs as possible. If you have any reviews from websites or even a review from one of Amazon's Hall of Fame reviewers be sure to list it in your description. This will add credibility to your book. Try to work as many keywords into your book description as is possible without making the descriptions sound contrived.

You're looking for a compromise here. Your book description will be read by Amazons search engine as well as humans so try to balance it accordingly. If you have a personal connection to the subject matter then include it but only after your bullet point presentation. If your book is about overcoming cancer and is based on your personal experiences then you should include that information in your description.

This is the book description that Ray Reynolds originally wrote for his heart failure book. It is one of the finest examples of how not to write a book description that I've ever seen. If this were cleaned up it would make a decent author biography but it says absolutely nothing about how this book will benefit the prospective buyer.

I'm a 66-year-old 5'8" 180lb. bodybuilder. During the last year I have had 4 different facelift procedures done in Thailand, a massive heart attack while under sedation followed by 2.5 hours of CPR and a one-week coma. A month later my weakened heart went into congestive failure so severe that I could not walk 15 feet without being out of breath.

Along the way I went through a divorce after being married for 30 years and 3 basal cell carcinomas. I should have died many times over but having decided that there was no viable up side to that strategy I did my research and found cures for all of my afflictions, well...except for the divorce, that one just keeps on giving. Only 5% of CPR recipients survive longer than 30 minutes.

That must put me in the 1% group. Only 50% of extended coma victims survive. 40% of all congestive heart failure patients die within the first year. I currently walk a mile to the gym every other day; lift the same weights as prior to my CHF and then walk back to my apartment. Additionally I walk a couple of more miles each day to shop or visit friends.

All of this is in Arequipa, Peru at an altitude of 7,500' where there is 17% less oxygen per breath. I'm a serial survivor who should have died many times over and I have been trying to analyze and quantify the why of it ever since."

Here's the revised book description that I wrote for him as it currently appears on his "Heart Failure" book's product page. Notice how the first header is in h2 text. It and its' sub header are the only text visible when a potential buyer lands on the product page. The main header makes a statement of fact that is designed to catch the person's attention and after a few seconds of thought draw him down to the sub header, which explains, why the header information is important.

The potential buyer then reads a bullet point list that itemizes the information contained within the book that might be of help to him. Afterwards they can read the less important details about the author's reason for writing the book if they so desire. At the end is a suggestion to purchase the book. Following it is the book description for the Cancer book as well.

"Our knowledge of human biology doubles every four years."

This makes it nearly impossible for physicians to stay current on the latest research in their own fields let alone in all of the others that directly effect their ability to properly treat their patients.

In this new book by Bio Researcher Ray Reynolds you will learn...

- How heart muscle cells have the ability to stay alive by hibernating when deprived of oxygen.

- The four nutrients needed to revive them after the coronary artery blockage has been removed.

- How to utilize minimum effective doses of heart medications to regulate your blood pressure and pulse.

- The mechanics and symptoms of heart failure.

- The prescription medication that is 30% more effective than enalapril and will be available in 2015.

These are just a few of the proven congestive heart failure healing strategies that Ray Reynolds discuses in his new book "Congestive Heart Failure Recovery". In it he provides a detailed presentation of the latest research data for preventing and treating heart failure.

Heart muscle cells are able to shut down and hibernate for extended periods of time. This allows them to easily survive on the small amount of oxygen that leaks past a coronary artery obstruction until it is removed. Unfortunately afterwards they are usually in a stunted condition that requires very high blood plasma levels of the the proper nutrients to allow them to regain normal function. This book will explain how to provide them with that nutrient rich environment that will return them to normal contractile function.

Reynolds is a 66 year old research biologist and lifelong body builder. This is the story of how congestive heart failure turned him into an invalid who could not walk more than twenty feet without gasping for breath and how he completely recovered from that condition in 6 months. An exhaustive list of the common supplements that took him from not being able to walk up a flight of stairs to running up them two steps at a time one week latter is included. This would be enough of a miracle by itself even if he were not currently living at 7,500 feet in the high sierras of southern Peru where there is 17 percent less oxygen per breath.

If you have congestive heart failure or know someone who does, the information in this book will be of great help. Granted Ray was in excellent physical condition prior to the heart attack and subsequent congestive heart failure but the research shows that nearly everyone, even people in their 70s who are bed ridden from heart failure show exponential improvement using this simple treatment protocol that a few knowledgeable cardiologists have used for the last 30 years.

If you or someone you know is currently suffering from heart failure this book will provide you with the latest research data that you will need to help treat it.

Every home library should have a copy

Samuel Davis - Editor, Plowboy Publications

"Our knowledge of human biology doubles every four years."

This makes it nearly impossible for physicians to stay current on the latest research in their own fields let alone in all of the others that directly effect their ability to properly treat their patients.

"In this new book by Bio Researcher Ray Reynolds you will learn..."

- Why 85% of all oncologist who are asked state that they would never do chemotherapy themselves.

- Why you should use anti-angiogenic medications to treat your tumor instead of chemotherapy.

- Which foods shrink tumors by preventing the formation of the blood vessels that feed them.

- Which two green teas when combined are 6 times more effective at preventing cancer than separately.

- Why people who drink 4 cups of coffee each day are 40% less likely to have cancer.

- A more recent study has conclusively proven that coffee combined with exercise enables your body to destroy twice as many cancer cells as either coffee or exercise by itself.

These are just a few of the hundreds of proven cancer fighting strategies that Bio Researcher Ray Reynolds discuses in his new book "Cancer Cures, The Latest Research". In it he provides a detailed presentation of the latest research data for preventing and treating Cancer. Instead of the usual one sided opinion favoring either mainstream or alternative care the author draws on his years of experience as a researcher to present the best of both disciplines.

If you or someone you know is currently suffering from cancer this book will provide you with the latest research data that you will need to treat it.

Get a copy for your home library today!

Samuel Davis - Editor, Plowboy Publications

The reason I'm able to use different size headers and bullet lists in my book descriptions is that I'm using what are called "Kindle simple HTML tags". These are very easy to learn and a description of their usage follows.

Headline tags. These create different size fonts.

<h1>Text</h1> This one is the largest
<h2>Text</h2>
<h3>Text</h3>
<h4>Text</h4>
<h5>Text</h5>
<h6>Text</h6> This one is the smallest

Text Formatting tags

Text Makes enclosed text bold

 Used at the end of a passage of text to produce a space and start of new parapraph.

Text Emphasizes text by making it italics.

<hr> Produces a horizontal line to divide text areas.

Text Makes enclosed text italic.

_{Text} Makes text into subscript.

^{Text} Makes text into superscript.

<u>Text</u> Makes text into underlined.

<strike>Text</strike> Makes text into strikethrough.

<p>Text</p> defines a paragraph of text creating a line break at the end.

List Tags

<ul> Used to start a bullet list.

</ul> Used to end a bullet list.

<ol> Used to start a numbered list.

</ol> Used to end a numbered list.

<li>Text</li> Used to indicate that the enclosed text is a list item.

Here are the same Book descriptions as before with the Kindle simple HTML tags that were used to format them. If you were to copy and paste it into your description entry window when you upload your book to KDP your book's description would be the same. All you need to do is change the text that is in between the HTML tags to the text for your book description.

If you want to test your coding prior to upload do the following.

Open a new TextEdit document on your Mac computer or Notepad on your Windows machine.

Make certain that your TextEdit or notepad document is set to "plain text" so that no hidden formatting characters will be transported into it.

Copy and paste your entire book description along with its' HTML tags into your plaintext document.

Now find the plain text document and change its suffix from .txt to .htm.

Double-click on it and it will open in your browser and be displayed just the same as it will look when viewed on your book's product page on Amazon.

If you need to make corrections change the .htm back to .txt and open it in notepad again to make the changes. Then reverse the process to view the changes in your browser.

Here is the exact book description that we uploaded to Ray's Cancer Cures book details page on KDP.

<h3>Our knowledge of human biology doubles every four years.</h3>

<p>This makes it nearly impossible for physicians to stay current on the latest research in their own fields let alone in all of the others that directly effect their ability to properly treat their patients.</p>

<h3>In this new book by Bio Researcher Ray Reynolds you will learn...</h3>

<ul>
<li>Why 85% of all oncologist who are asked state that they would never do chemotherapy themselves.</li>
<li>Why you should use anti-angiogenic medications to treat your tumor instead of chemotherapy.</li>

<li>Which foods shrink tumors by preventing the formation of the blood vessels that feed them.</li>
<li>Which two green teas when combined are 6 times more effective at preventing cancer than separately.</li>
<li>Why people who drink 4 cups of coffee each day are 40% less likely to have cancer.</li>
<li>A more recent study has conclusively proven that coffee combined with exercise enables your body to destroy twice as many cancer cells as either coffee or exercise by itself.</li>
</ul>

<p> These are just a few of the hundreds of proven cancer fighting strategies that Bio Researcher Ray Reynolds discuses in his new book "Cancer Cures, The Latest Research". In it he provides a detailed presentation of the latest research data for preventing and treating Cancer. Instead of the usual one sided opinion favoring either mainstream or alternative care the author draws on his years of experience as a researcher to present the best of both disciplines.</p>

<p> If you or someone you know is currently suffering from cancer this book will provide you with the latest research data that you will need to treat it.</p>

<h2>Get a copy for your home library today!</h2>

<p> Samuel Davis - Editor, Plowboy Publications</p>

10 LAUNCHING YOUR EBOOK

This is the chapter "Where the rubber meets the road" or "The shit hits the fan" depending on your point of view. I will first present the standard book promotion that everyone recommends and then provide you with an analysis of why it doesn't work. There are two different types of Kindle promotions that you can run if you are a member of KDP Select. They are the Kindle free promo and the Kindle countdown.

There are a couple of very good reasons for not using the Kindle countdown. The first is that your book has to be listed for at least a month without price change prior to using it. That is just too long to wait between publishing your book and launching it. The other reason is that I've never had any success using it.

The recommended book launch is usually organized as follows:

The Kindle Free promotion followed by $0.99 combo
Obviously you will not get paid for any of the free downloads that occur during the five day free promotion of your book. This would not be a problem if there were any real benefit to this philanthropy, but there isn't. The theory is that this process will establish your

book's initial ranking within the Kindle system and help the search engine determine what reader demographic to recommend your book to.

The proponents of this type of launch believe that the Amazon's search engine algorithms will be able to analyze all of these free downloads and determine which buyer demographic to recommend your book to in the future when the promotion ends and your book is being sold at its normal price. Let's examine this concept logically.

Every day there are millions of people who visit the Kindle store for the sole purpose of downloading free books. Most of them will never read the books they download. They simply click on anything that they believe might be of possible interest to them sometime in the far future. They might download five video gaming books followed by your book and then 10 romance novels of various types and after that a few science fiction books and then several books on conspiracy theories. Please explain to me how that will help your book's ranking and demographic profile with the search engine?

Another problem is that no matter how many free downloads your book gets during the initial promotion none of them will count towards your ranking when it switches over to the top 100 paid list after five days of this free promo insanity. Ray Reynolds did an Amazon free 5-day promotion for his cancer cures book when he first launched it on July 15 2015. Here's the company it was keeping afterwards!

Cancer Cures customers who viewed this item also viewed list
Improve Your Eyesight Naturally
Facial Exercises
Blink, the Power of Thinking Without Thinking
22 Smart Ways to Increase Your Intelligence
Learn to be a Virtual Recruiter

How to Learn Faster With Mind Maps
Acupuncture for Beginners
Vision Correction in Home
Heal Without Regrets
How to Make Strong Teeth
Hacking Now!
Critical Thinking
Amazing Abilities of Your Magical Mind

After the latest $.99 promotion on September 6 2015 these were the books that were on his "Customers who bought this item also bought" list

9/11
Pay Attention, Say Thank you
Natural antibiotics
Harry Watt, Bounty Hunter
Weresisters
Feral Planet
Lovers, Players and the Seducer
Fawn
Opiate Addiction
A chasing after the wind
Milf Money

Not the best of company for a serious book about curing cancer to hang out with.

What the pundits then recommend is that you offer your book for an extended period at $0.99 to "rocket it up" to the top of the 100 paid chart for its' category. And UP it does go. Unfortunately it immediately comes back down again like a bad case of parachute failure! Below is a screenshot of the initial 5-day Amazon free promotion (green) followed by about 10 days of $0.99 bottom feeding. He then changed the price to $2.99 and the sales dried up to nada. Same thing happened for the $0.99 promo on September 6 2015. Straight up to the moon then straight back down again.

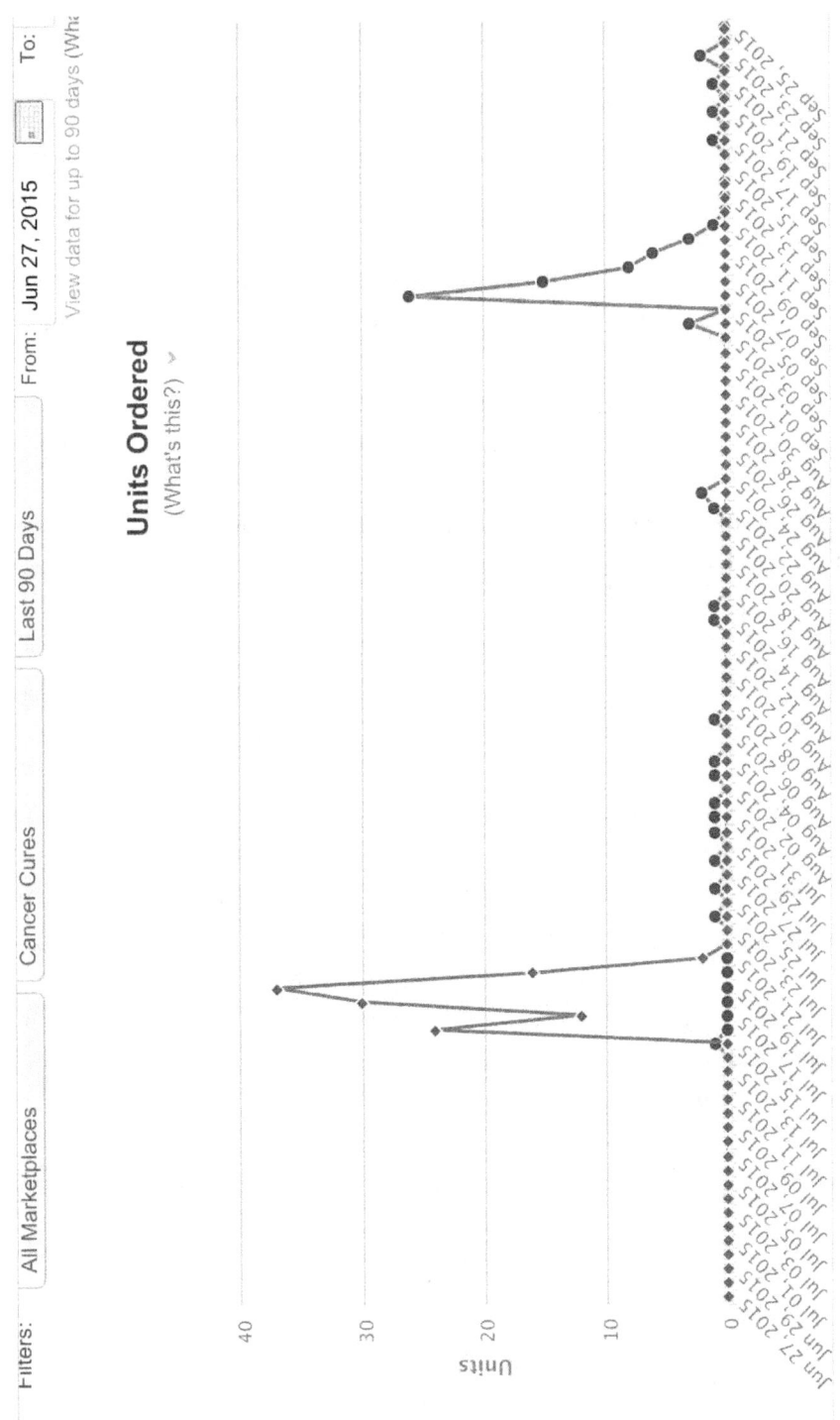

So if all of the so called experts recommend this particular strategy and claim that it actually works for them, but it hasn't worked for either of these books we need to determine the why of it. The first question that I would ask is have any authors ever written a really good book in a popular category and then simply uploaded it and done nothing to launch or promote it? I have read of a few cases of this happening and some of them take right off on their own and become best sellers with no post upload launch and no promotion.

I honestly believe that what happens is that there are so many books on how to write and publish a Kindle ebook that every new author reads at least three of them before publishing his book. Since all of these books recommended the free promo followed by the $.99 sale. Every new author does it that way without considering the possibility of taking the contrarian path and doing no promotion to see what will happen. The result of this is that whenever these books take off and are really successful it reflects well on that type of promotion whether it was instrumental in selling the book or not.

If the book doesn't sell well then the author simply assumes that he wrote a bad book that no one likes. There is however a third possibility, which I believe covers many cases of failed books such as the two we are examining. That is, the author has written a book about a subject in which there is very little interest. It doesn't necessarily mean that the book was poorly written it simply means that the new author does not understand how to market a book that has low demand. The marketing strategy is very different.

I honestly believe that the books, which we are examining, fall into this category. Remember in the chapter on copywriting when I said that the sale of any product is very much dependent upon the demographic to whom the product is being marketed? The demographic that most often suffers from heart failure and cancer are older people who are not very high-tech.

If a younger member of their family is not being proactive and trying to source the information on the Internet or attempting to find books on Kindle, then the older person will probably not know that this source of information is even available let alone know how to use a computer in order to access it. They will more often be interested in a traditional paperback book rather than an e-book.

Back in July when I first decided to try and help Ray out the first thing that I did was to upload a copy of each of his books to CreateSpace so that they would be available in paperback as well as electronic version. At the same time we reworked both his book description and uploaded new professionally designed covers. The end result of this is that for September he has sold 10 copies of each book in paperback at a much higher royalty. He has only sold 22 electronic versions of the same two books on KDP. That is a little more than 100% gain in total sales by publishing the same books as paperbacks on CreateSpace. Obviously the demographic that these books is targeting prefers to read a hard copy rather than an ebook. We will study this phenomenon in greater detail later.

Search engine insanity
Amazon's search engine is unimaginably efficient at establishing relationships between buyer search phrases and book information in order to determine which books it should recommend to that customer. Unfortunately common sense is not one of its virtues. Amazon's search engine is desperate to find a match for just about anything in its database. For example:

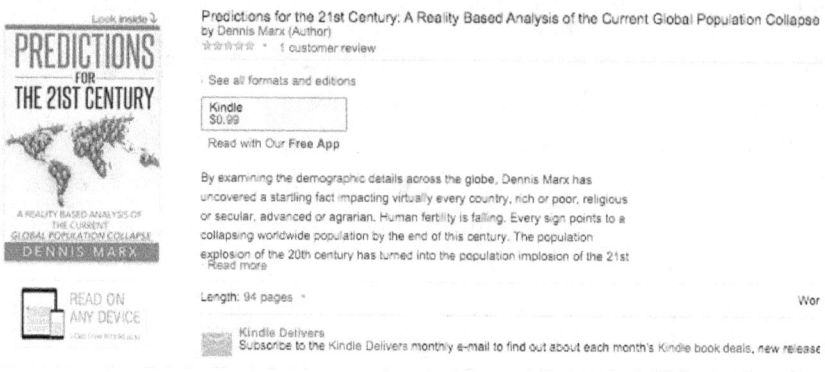

Predictions for the 21st Century: A Reality Based Analysis of the Current Global Population Collapse
by Dennis Marx (Author)
★★★★★ · 1 customer review

· See all formats and editions

Kindle
$0.99

Read with Our Free App

By examining the demographic details across the globe, Dennis Marx has uncovered a startling fact impacting virtually every country, rich or poor, religious or secular, advanced or agrarian. Human fertility is falling. Every sign points to a collapsing worldwide population by the end of this century. The population explosion of the 20th century has turned into the population implosion of the 21st
Read more

Length: 94 pages ·   Wor

Kindle Delivers
Subscribe to the Kindle Delivers monthly e-mail to find out about each month's Kindle book deals, new release

Customers Who Viewed This Item Also Viewed

Cancer Cures: A synergistic approach to cancer
› Ray Reynolds
★★★★☆ 11
Kindle Edition
$2.99

This is a screenshot of the landing page of another friend's book that I just finished editing and publishing for him. As soon as I had published it I made up and started maintaining a spreadsheet that contained all of the possible search phrases a person might use for locating this type of book. Each day for three days I had recorded the book's position in the search results for each of those search phrases. This of course required me to search for and click on it about 30 times per day.

Interspersed throughout this process I was also clicking on the cancer cures book in order to determine how well it was doing during its paid promotion. The end result was that Amazon's search engine established a connection between the two books. The information it is presenting is perfectly accurate. The only customer on Amazon who seemed to be interested in the predictions book did indeed view the cancer cures book as well but it was not because he was interested in buying either one. I was simply doing research that involved selecting each book in turn numerous times.

Does this suggest a way that we can game Amazon's search engine system?

1. Buy the best selling book in our particular category that is relatively inexpensive and then buy our own book that we just uploaded and or having a friend do this.

2. When someone clicked on that other book would ours then appear in that books "Also bought list causing prospective customers of the other book to examine and possibly buy ours as well thereby strengthening that connection between the two of them? Then when someone selects the bestseller our book will pop up in the also bought list for that book. I haven't had time to test this theory but it appears to have worked in this particular case.

This shows how single-mindedly desperate the search engine is when making connections between search phrases as well as between different books that are viewed or bought by the same individual. What it is trying to do here is to determine what particular type of customer wants to view a particular category of book. If it does not have a large enough sample of purchases or viewings of a particular book especially if it is a newly published one it will make connections that may not be appropriate.

As far as I'm concerned this is the main reason never to run a free promotion of your book. As I said a few pages back the free book gremlins will make even the best-conceived free promo into a search engine train wreck. Amazon's poor search engine will be totally confused and decide that your book on a health related topic should be catalogued with books about Tesla conspiracy theories.

If at the same time you decide to give your book a cute title like my friend Ray did when he first published his cancer book then you really are setting yourself up for disaster. His book was originally published under the title "Cancer Relativity" with the subtitle "A Unified Theory". The result was that when anyone searched for Einstein or his theory of relativity Ray's book on cancer would appear on the first or second page of search results. People who were looking for information about Einstein's Theory of relativity would find the title "Cancer Relativity" interesting and click on it only to discover that it wasn't about the topic they were looking for and then go on to select other books that were.

The end result was that even though Ray's cancer book was located in the "Oncology" category the search engine when handling search phrases would ignore that and recommend it to people searching for information about Einstein's theory of relativity as well as other books about the Nikola Tesla conspiracies. This type of search engine confusion is difficult to cure once it becomes established. Avoid it by developing titles that are strictly descriptive of the book's actual contents and very short.

Another reason for being very literal when naming your book is that the Amazon search engine gives preferential treatment to books with titles that contain a major keyword that is always used when searching for that type of book. If your book is about cancer and its' title contains the word "Cancer" then your book will be listed ahead of any other books on that subject that do not have the word cancer in their title.

It does not matter how many times the author included the word cancer in his keyword phrases. The same is true for the subtitle. This is why you often see a book whose subtitle runs on for a paragraph and contains nothing but keywords. The author is trying to game the system. This should be avoided, as it looks very unprofessional to a potential buyer. Try to craft your title in such a way that it uses the key search phrases without seeming contrived.

The screenshot below shows another search engine anomaly. This one is of the cancer cures book's landing page immediately after I ran the three-day Booksbutterfly.com $.99 promotion. Prior to this its' "Customers who bought this item also bought" listing contained about 40 different books none of which had anything to do with cancer and likewise none of which actually linked back to the Cancer Cures book.

Cancer Cures: A synergistic approach to cancer prevention and treatment
by Ray Reynolds * (Author)
⭐⭐⭐⭐☆ * 11 customer reviews

· See all 2 formats and editions

Kindle $0.00 kindleunlimited	Paperback $9.99

Subscribers read for free
$2.99 to buy
prime Borrow for free *

2 Used from $9.19
8 New from $8.65

There is no other medical subject about which more information has been written with so little positive results. After a total expenditure of more than $2 trillion since 1970 with the sole purpose of finding a viable cure for cancer its' rate has more than doubled. The medical care establishment refers to anything except
· Read more

Length: 199 pages *

 Descubre Kindle Flash: una selección de eBooks con descuentos de hast
Suscríbete a la newsletter de Kindle Flash y recibe, cada día, en tu correo elect

Customers Who Bought This Item Also Bought

| Natural Antibiotics: 30 of the Most Powerful Natural...
Janice Blair
⭐⭐⭐⭐⭐ 7
Kindle Edition
$2.99 | Harry Watt, Bounty Hunter: 2150 AD - And Harry's Life...
›Rob Guy
⭐⭐⭐⭐⭐ 26
Kindle Edition
$0.99 | Weresisters: A Novel for Young Adults
›John Patrick Kennedy
⭐⭐⭐⭐⭐ 38
Kindle Edition
$0.99 | Lovers, Players & The Seducer: The Storm is Coming...
›J. A. Jackson
⭐⭐⭐⭐⭐ 30
Kindle Edition
$0.99 | 101 Amazing Facts
›Jack Goldstein
⭐⭐⭐⭐☆ 91
Kindle Edition
$0.00 |

Now all of those unrelated books have been eliminated and have been replaced with three fiction books, which have nothing to do with cancer or any other health related subject and one book about amazing facts. The last book about natural antibiotics is definitely health-related and when we click through to its product page it actually does have the "Cancer Cures" book listed in its "Customers who bought" section. So that particular one is logical and working the way it should. Each book lists the other as having been bought by the same customer.

Notice that the three fiction books are $.99 and the facts book is free. These other books were probably listed in the same promotional email that the cancer book was on. In other words the email recipients of the promotion clicked on the Cancer Cures book and bought it and then purchased some of the other books on the same email list that had been sent to them. This caused the search engine to link these books together with the cancer cures book.

My book launch method

While I do not believe that any form of book promotion will be successful in the long run for maintaining a book's ranking within its category I do believe that an initial $0.99 offering through various paid email lists might be beneficial in elevating your book to a position in its' category where the search engine will decide to help with its' promotion.

This is particularly true for a new book that has just been uploaded. For the first month the Amazon search engine gives preferential treatment to a new book in any of the categories. It will give it an unfair vantage over the older establish books so that readers are continually being exposed to new offerings in the upper ranks of those categories instead of always seeing the same old books. My method of promoting a new book is very simple and straightforward.

1. Set your book's price to $0.99. By doing this you guarantee that only people who are seriously interested in that type of book will download it. This will also immediately move your book up the paid 100-bestseller list in your category. At this price point buyers will also be more inclined to leave you a good review if they enjoy reading your book. Paid reviews are worth ten times as much for moving your book up the rating scale as unpaid reviews in the kindle system.

2. Go to www.booksbutterfly.com and click on the buy a paid slot button near the top of the page.

3. Go to the silver 50 column and click its' buy button. Fill out the form and click buy.

4. The owner of this promotion service will check to make certain that your book fits the criteria needed to be included in one of his email lists. If it does he will email you a PayPal link to make payment.

The owner of this e-book promotion service has been a major developer of gaming applications for years and because of this has a very large email list. This has resulted in a 130,000 person email list of potential buyers of bargain ebooks.

Essentially what he is doing is charging you $1.00 per book that is downloaded during the three-day promotion. If you pay $50 he guarantees you 50 paid $0.99 downloads. If your book promotion only generates 25 he will refund you $25 to be used on your next promotion. If you receive more than 50 paid downloads you do not pay any extra. This is the best deal I have found anywhere for promoting an ebook.

When I set up the promotion for Ray's cancer book the owner figured that I would receive 30 - 60 paid downloads over the three-day promotion. The book only received 49 downloads. Since I had purchased the silver 50 plan he refunded me a dollar. For the predictions book he only charged me $25 upfront for the silver service because he thought it would only generate about 25 sales for that type of book. It generated only 22 so he refunded $3.

The difference between a niche, a category and a search phrase
These three terms are often confused with each other. They are in reality completely different and until you understand that difference you will never be able to market your book effectively. The best way to show the difference is with the following screenshots.

Best Sellers in Demography

Top 100 Paid   **Top 100 Free**

1.	2.	3.

Date-onomics: How Dating Became a Lop...	Predictions for the 21st Century: A R...	English: Learn English In 7 Days! - T...
by Jon Birger	by Dennis Marx	by Dagny Taggart
★★★★☆ (10)	★★★★★ (1)	★★★★☆ (24)
Kindle Edition	Kindle Edition	Kindle Edition
$9.49	$0.99	$3.99

Here are the top 3 books in the Demography category.

The number 1 book is very successful, by a popular author and is published by a traditional publishing house in both hardcover and paperback. At first it appears to be a dating book that should not be in this category but on closer inspection of its contents and description it reveals itself to be an excellent treatment of the demographic aspects of dating. It also has one of the best cover designs I have ever seen.

This book's niche is Dating Demographics and its' category is Demography. Its' search phrases would be words like "Dating Demographics"

The number 2 book is by my friend Dennis Marx who requested that I edit and publish it for him. Obviously it should be here in the Demographics category as well. Its' niche is Population Demographics. Its' category is Demography. The search phrases I set up for it were listed and discussed in chapter four.

The number 3 book is about learning English as a second language (ESL). The only reason the author placed this book in an unpopular category like Demography instead of the Languages category where it should be is that it will always be in the top 10 books in the demography category and because of this the Amazon search engine will consider it a top 10 best seller and promote it as such. It gets worse than this - much worse!

Here is one of the least competitive categories in the Kindle Store. There are only nine books in it and none of them have anything to do with Cardiovascular Disease! What they do have in common is that all of these authors understand the principle of placing your book in the least competitive category you can find. They are also disingenuous enough to not care that their books have nothing to do with the category subject mater! The number one book only has an ABSR of 250,000. That would not get you number 100 position on most top 100 paid lists!

Some of you are probably wondering why Ray's book on heart failure recovery is not listed here. It would be the perfect category for it and at least its' subject mater would be appropriate. The problem is I can't find this category in the KDP version of the category lists on his book's detail entry page! The nomenclature is so different between the KDP category list and the Amazon category list that I could not locate it. I emailed KDP Support and asked them to move his book for him.

Below are before and after screen shots of this category's book contents. Rays heart failure book will probably be number one forever.

‹ Any Department
‹ Kindle Store
 ‹ Kindle eBooks
  ‹ Medical eBooks
   Diseases
    AIDS & HIV
    Brain
    Cardiovascular
    Diabetes
    Digestive Organs
    Extremities
    Viral

Best Sellers in Cardiovascular Diseases

Top 100 Paid   Top 100 Free

1.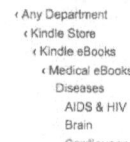
Dash Diet: Beginners Quick Start Guid...
by J.J. Lewis
★★★★☆ ☑ (24)
Kindle Edition
$3.09

2.
Man Boobs!! Step by step Guide to Get...
by Shawn Rashid
★★★★☆ ☑ (12)
Kindle Edition
$9.99

3.
Metabolism : Learn How to Super Charg...
by Shawn Rashid
★★★★☆ ☑ (10)
Kindle Edition
$9.99

4.
THE MIRACULOUS CURE FOR INFINITE AILM...
by SRI R
★★★★☆ ☑ (2)
Kindle Edition
$0.99

5.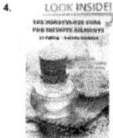
Acid Reflux Disease: Natural Cures an...
by Shawn Rashid
★★★★☆ ☑ (11)
Kindle Edition
$9.99

6.
Say Goodbye to Your Double Chin Forever
by Shawn Rashid
★★★★☆ ☑ (13)
Kindle Edition
$9.97

7.
Smoothie Recipes for Breakfast: Smoot...
by Shawn Rashid
★★★★★ ☑ (9)
Kindle Edition
$9.99

8.
Say Goodbye to Your Double Chin Forever
by Shawn Rashid
★★★★★ ☑ (13)
Kindle Edition
$9.97

9.
Belly Fat Blast: How to Burn Off Bell...
by Shawn Rashid
★★★★★ ☑ (1)
Kindle Edition
$9.99

The screen shot below was taken 12 hours later.

110

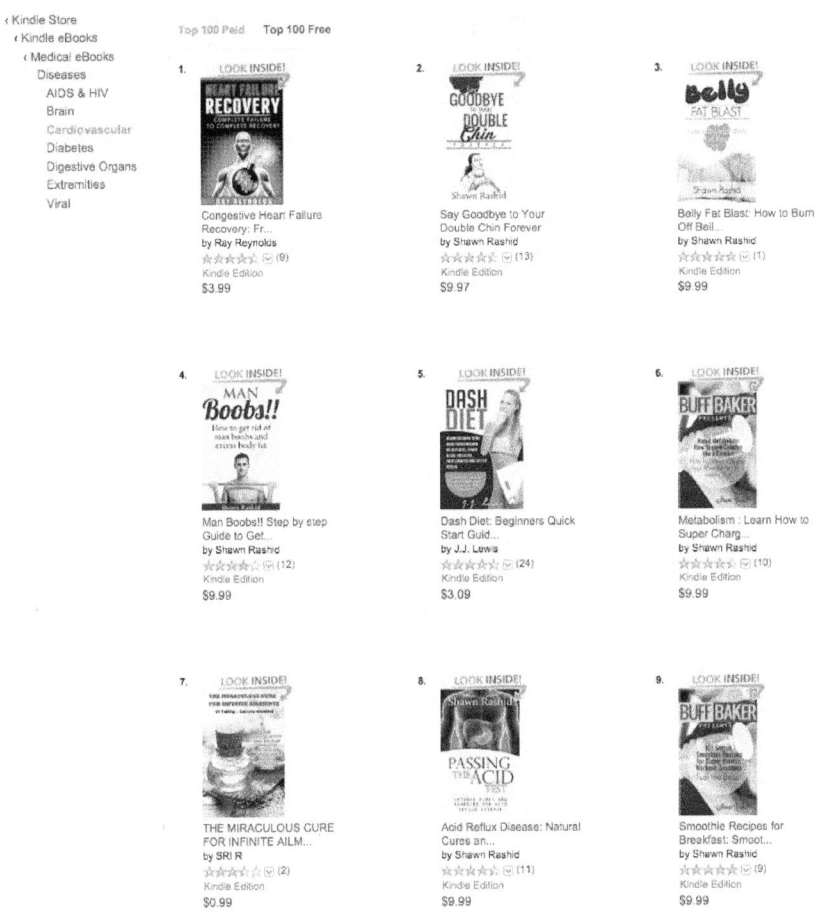

Starting to get the idea? Please do not abuse this concept by placing your latest Bondage and Discipline novel in the Italian cookbook section even if the story does take place in an Italian restaurant!

On the next page is a screen shot of the spreadsheet I made up to track the Cancer Cures $0.99 promotion that started on Sept. 6 2015.

O Rank is the overall store rank
R Chemo is the rank in the Chemotherapy Category
R Cancer is the rank in the General Cancer Category
BB .99 are the days that the 3-day booksbutterfly.com $0.99 promotion ran.

Hotzippy .99 is another ebook promotion site that I did a two-day follow up promotion on.

Cancer ebook

	Date	Time	O Rank	R Chemo	R Cancer	Sales	Promo
1	Date	Time	O Rank	R Chemo	R Cancer	Sales	Promo
2	9/6/15	24hrs	10k		3	26	BB .99
3	9/7/15	12am	10k		3		BB .99
4	9/7/15	1pm	10k		3		
5	9/7/15	2pm	10k		3		
6	9/7/15	3pm	12k		3		
7	9/7/15	7pm	13k		3		
8	9/7/15	9pm	14k		3		
9	9/7/15	11pm	13.5k		3	15	
10	9/8/15	3pm	17.7k		4		BB .99
11	9/8/15	4pm	18.5k		5		
12	9/8/15	6pm	17.5k		3		
13	9/8/15	8pm	16.7k		4		
14	9/8/15	11pm	19k		4	8	Hotzippy .99
15	9/9/15	7am	18.6k		5		Hotzippy .99
16	9/9/15	9am	21.2k		5		
17	9/9/15	10am	21.4k		5		
18	9/9/15	12pm	20.7k		3		
19	9/9/15	2pm	22k		5		
20	9/9/15	5pm	23.4k		6		
21	9/9/15	7pm	25k		7		
22	9/9/15	11pm	25k		7	6	
23	9/10/15	7am	32k		11		
24	9/10/15	10am	27.5k		7		
25	9/10/15	12pm	29k		8		
26	9/10/15	2pm	31k		9		
27	9/10/15	5pm	32k		10		
28	9/10/15	8pm	30.4k		9		
29	9/10/15	9pm	39k		9		
30	9/10/15	11pm	36.5k		11	5	
31	9/11/15	7am	47k		15		
32	9/11/15	9am	39k		14		
33	9/11/15	1pm	40k		13		
34	9/11/15	3pm	42k		14		
35	9/11/15	5pm	44k		15		
36	9/11/15	7pm	47.5k		16		
37	9/11/15	9pm	50.8k		16	1	
38	9/11/15	11pm	54k		17		

On September 17 we change the price from $0.99 to $3.99. Two weeks Prior to running this promotion we had also change to the new cover design as well as upgrading the book description. We also changed the second category to Chemotherapy so you can see how selecting a noncompetitive category for a book's second category can exponentially improve its ranking.

You can also see the rate at which the book's rank drops when no sales are made. Increasing the price from $0.99 to $3.99 has not affected the sales volume at all. This indicates to me that the most important factor in the success of your book is its' presentation and quality not your promotion strategy.

It is interesting that if a group of people is visually presented with a book that they were not looking for they will buy it even if the subject mater was the furthest thing from their minds. This all comes back to the visibility issue and demonstrates why it is so important that your book has good visibility within Amazon. This is one advantage that a real bookstore has over a virtual one.

When a customer walks around in a bookstore his sensory input is different. He will see the covers and titles of books on varying subjects that he would not normally have thought to look for on Amazon. He can then take a look at those books and decide to purchase one. On amazon he will only see books on subjects that he enters into the Kindle Store search bar. As with every other product the sales volume of your book will depend on whether or not customers are given the opportunity to see it. This aspect of ebook shopping is the main limiting factor for sales volume.

Notice how even when the Cancer Cures book is book 141 in the General Cancer category it is still in the top ten books in the Chemotherapy category and being promoted as such.

		Time	O Rank	R Chemo	R Cancer	Sales	Promo
77							
78	9/17/15	7am	241k		112		$.99 > $3.99
79	9/17/15	9am	245k		125		
80	9/17/15	12pm	245k		125		
81	9/17/15	2pm	245k		125	1	
82	9/17/15	5pm	244k	11	124		
83	9/17/15	7pm	92k	4	35		
84	9/17/15	9pm	113k	4	48		
85	9/17/15	11pm	126k	4	54		
86	9/18/15	7am	100k	3	38		
87	9/18/15	10am	118k	4	43		
88	9/18/15	3pm	133k	5	55		
89	9/18/15	6pm	148k	5	63		
90	9/18/15	7am	197k	7	91		
91	9/19/15	11am	202k	8	93		
92	9/19/15	3pm	202k	8	90	1	
93	9/19/15	6pm	203k	8	94		
94	9/19/15	8pm	206k	9	91		
95	9/20/15	8am	84k	3	30		
96	9/20/15	2pm	94k	3	32		
97	9/20/15	8pm	115k	3	31		
98	9/20/15	9pm	66k	2	25		
99	9/21/15	6am	66k	2	25		
100	9/21/15	12pm	144k	3	55		
101	9/21/15	9pm	158k	4	66	1	
102	9/21/15	2pm	139k	5	42		
103	9/22/15	10pm	170k	6	84	1	
104	9/23/15	7am	202k	4	95		
105	9/23/15	7pm	90k	3	31	1	
106	9/24/15	6am	75k	3	26		
107	9/25/15	7am	139k	6	55		
108	9/25/15	1pm	121k	4	47		
109	9/25/15	5pm	135k	4	58		
110	9/25/15	8pm	143k	5	62		
111	9/25/15	10pm	153k	5	68		
112	9/26/15	6am	185k	5	88		
113	9/26/15	11am	203k	6	99		
114	9/27/15	7am	246k	8	131		
115	9/27/15	10am	255k	10	143		

Congestive Heart Failure book

No promotion was done for the Heart Failure book. I did not want to ruin the connections that had been made over the last few months with other appropriate books on its' also bought list. We changed its' book description and cover design September 4th. The reason that there is a jump from 64 to 18 in its' category rank during the morning of the first day is two sales were made just prior to midnight the previous day and because of system latency it did not change the category rank until the next day.

C Rank = Category Rank

O Rank = Overall Store Rank

	Date	Time	O Rank	C Rank	Sales	Promo
39						
40	9/12/15	6am	212k	64		
41	9/12/15	10am	90k	18		
42	9/12/15	1pm	96k	18		
43	9/12/15	4pm	114k	21		
44	9/12/15	7pm	127k	28		
45	9/12/15	9pm	140k	35		
46	9/12/15	11pm	166k	50		
47	9/12/15	8am	212k	59		
48	9/13/15	10am	218k	58		
49	9/13/15	12pm	222k	53		
50	9/13/15	4pm	226k	56		
51	9/13/15	6pm	231k	61		
52	9/13/15	8pm	243k	67		
53	9/13/15	11pm	250k	69		
54	9/14/15	7am	281k	78		
55	9/14/15	11am	295k	81		
56	9/14/15	1pm	298k	81		
57	9/14/15	4pm	300k	80		
58	9/14/15	6pm	302k	83		
59	9/14/15	8pm	306k	86		
60	9/14/15	10pm	308k	87		
61	9/14/15	11pm	309k	88		
62	9/15/15	6am	327k	98		
63	9/15/15	12pm	334k	98		
64	9/15/15	3pm	335k	95		
65	9/15/15	6pm	336k	99		
66	9/15/15	8pm	339k	103	1	
67	9/15/15	10pm	343k	104		
68	9/16/15	6am	121k	29		
69	9/16/15	8am	140k	34		
70	9/16/15	11am	165k	38		
71	9/16/15	1pm	174k	40		
72	9/16/15	3pm	183k	41		
73	9/16/15	5pm	200k	48		
74	9/16/15	10pm	221k	58		
75	9/17/15	7am	263k	80		
76	9/17/15	9am	277k	84		
77	9/17/15	12pm	282k	85	1	
78	9/17/15	2pm	133k	30		
79	9/17/15	5pm	151k	39		
80	9/17/15	9pm	174k	50		
81	9/17/15	11pm	187k	55		

Adrian Saunders

11 POST LAUNCH PROMOTION

After the initial launch promotion is over and your book is selling well your work is not over. You will still need to promote it in the future when sales start to lag. This chapter will concern itself with various ways to promote an e-book after it has been listed for a while and your sales are starting to deteriorate. I will only list and describe techniques that provide the greatest return for time and money invested. There are several others such as Twitter and Facebook promotion but really they're just not worth the effort.

1. Write more books

This is without a doubt the simplest and most effective method of increasing your book sales. The more books you write the more you have to sell! This is especially true if you are able to serialize your books so that if a customer reads one of them he will have a tendency to purchase others in the series if he enjoyed the first. This technique is a given with fiction writers. Almost inevitably they write a series of books all of which deal with the same characters and basic storyline throughout the series, which may consist of as many as twelve books. A smaller version of this technique consists of three books and is referred to as a trilogy.

If the reader really enjoyed reading the first book in the series when he gets to the last page and discovers your list of additional books within that series he will undoubtedly click through and purchase the next book in the series. A very useful tool for encouraging this is to include the first chapter of the next book in the series at the end of the current book so that the reader can get started on the next book even before he buys it. This will force him to make that additional purchase so he can finish the story.

This technique is equally effective for nonfiction as well. Two examples would be a series of books explaining how to design, develop and promote websites. There are many book series on how to write novels. The first book could be an overview of the entire novel writing process followed by a dozen books explaining all of the details concerning character development, plot development, how to create interesting opening chapter paragraphs, examples of different types of dialogue etc.

2. Book Bundles

Once you have written a series of books, whether fiction or nonfiction, you can bundle those related books together. This allows you to make a big sale all at once while discounting each book in the bundle so that the purchaser gets a good deal as well. It would be the equivalent of a volume discount. If you are bundling a three-book trilogy you might sell the three books for the price of two. You would continue to sell each of those books separately as before so that someone who only wanted one of the books could purchase it separately. This also increases the number of listings for that series on Amazon's search engine. If you have a series of six books you could divide them into two bundles of three. You would then have eight opportunities instead of six for people to locate that particular work.

The bundling process consists of creating a new manuscript for upload that contains all the books in that bundle with a single table of contents that would provide access to all three books contained in the bundle. In this particular case you would probably use "Heading

1" for the title of each individual book and link each of them to the title page of each of the books in that single manuscript. "Heading 2" would be used for listing the chapters in each of those books. Having created this new combined manuscript you would then upload it to your KDP account and publish it just like a new single volume book.

You should definitely change your cover image to what is called a 3-D box set style image. You can get this done on fiverr.com for $5-$10. You might also use a banner that says "Three books for the price of two". You have to make it absolutely clear which books are included in the bundle so that former purchasers of one or two of the books do not inadvertently buy those same books in the bundle. This can lead to negative reviews or requests for refunds.

3. Temporary price reduction

This is probably the simplest way of re-promoting an ebook. All you need to do is go to your bookshelf and click on your books price that's listed there. You will be taken to your pricing page where you can change the price to whatever you want. Scroll down to the bottom and check the box stating that you have the right to publish this book and click the publish button. Offering a book at a price of $.99 for a few days will boost your paid category ranking and consequently the visibility and desirability of your book sufficiently to make it worth the minor financial loss.

4. Developing relationships with other authors

If two or more authors can manage to cooperate with one another it will greatly improve both of their book sales. This cooperation can be in the form of cross promotion of one another's books as well as the exchange of ideas and techniques that will improve both authors writings.

The other benefit of this type of professional relationship is that the various authors can cross promote the other's books using one another's email lists so that your targeting a large group of people who are specifically interested in books on that particular subject matter. Another very powerful aspect is that a group of authors can get together and support one another's book launches by downloading and then reviewing the others books.

6. Publish a CreateSpace version of your book

This is Amazon's print-on-demand (POD) paperback division and if you will take the time to upload your manuscript to them along with the proper cover art they will make your e-book available in paperback version for people who prefer that format. The reason that this will boost your e-book sales is that Amazon will link your paperback version to your e-book version and its' price will appear on your book's product page next to the Kindle price.

This means that there will be two prices on your e-book page one will be the e-book price and the other will be the much higher paperback price. This will convince potential customers that they're getting a great deal by buying the ebook over the print version. The fact that the author has published a "real" book as well as an e-book version lends credibility to the author as well. For those who prefer it this will also provide the option of buying the paperback version instead of the ebook. This will boost your sales revenue by as much as 50% per book especially if the book appeals primarily to an older demographic.

When someone orders a create space copy of your e-book Amazon will print, assemble, trim and ship that e-book to the customer within one day. You can even order books for yourself at a discount so that they will cost only $2-$4. These are great to hand out to both family and business associates. Also an autographed copy is the ultimate business card to leave with a prospective client, as it will lend you an incredible amount of credibility. These books can be printed with color illustrations and images as well although it will cost significantly more.

It is a requirement of Amazon that your e-book price must be at least 20% less than the price of the physical version for you to continue receiving a 70% royalty for your Kindle book.

7. Translating your book for foreign markets.

There are many translators offering their services on fiverr.com, odesk.com and elance.com. The cost of translation is $250 to $350 per 10,000 words. Be aware that 80% of all ebooks are sold in English so this will only be profitable if you have a very high volume book in the US and British markets.

8. Testing your e-book parameters.

The primary elements of your e-book's composition and presentation that affect its' sale are:

1. Its price,
2. The cover art
3. The title and subtitle
4. Its' description.

The first thing that you will need to do is wait at least a month after your e-book's launch before you start experimenting with different titles, covers and descriptions. This will allow its sales figures to stabilize so that you will have a baseline to judge the success of your changes against. Of course you also must only conduct tests on one element of your books presentation at a time otherwise you will not know which change caused the increase or decrease in sales. Each of your tests should be at least one week in length so that you can gather a meaningful quantity of data from which to determine the viability of the change that you made.

Optimize the Price

According to Amazon's calculations you will maximize your royalties by pricing your book at $2.99. If your price is lower you will sell more books but you will only receive a 35% royalty so obviously that is a loser unless you happen to be trying to promote your book and raise its' ranking within its category. If you price it higher then you will make more money in royalties per book but of course your sales volume will probably drop.

There are of course always exceptions to the general rule so if you're really interested in experimenting you can raise your price to say $3.99 and see if it generates more total income for you. It might be that for your type of ebook a higher price is considered normal, which might result in greater profit and the same number of sales at the higher prices as you were receiving at the lower one. When we raised the prices of Ray's books from $2.99 to $3.99 there was no noticeable reduction in volume of sales.

The Cover

There is no prohibition against uploading a different cover so long as the title and subtitle on it are approximately the same as the title and subtitle listed for your book. If you change the title and subtitle of your book itself you will also need to upload a new cover, which reflects that title and subtitle change as well to avoid rejection when your new upload is reviewed. The reviewers are not overly strict about this so minor differences will probably be tolerated.

The Title and subtitle

There is no prohibition against changing either the title or subtitle of a Kindle ebook. You can do it as often as you want and it will not effect its listing in any way. All of the reviews and other pertinent information are linked to its ASIN number and not to its title. This is a very powerful tool for judging the effects those different titles and subtitles have on customer perception of your book. If you change your title or subtitle using words that better describe the contents of your book it will help with that books ranking and expose it to more customers. So the title and subtitle are two of the most important of your book elements to adjust.

The Description

When changing your description be sure to save the old copy just in case the new one doesn't work as well as you thought it would. Other than that this one is fairly straightforward. If you notice that you forgot an important selling point you can go back and edit it anytime by simply clicking on the appropriate book cover's edit details button in your bookshelf, which will take you to the first upload page where you can change it.

The reports section of your KDP bookshelf will provide you with a running total of your daily sales so you can accurately tabulate the results. If done properly in a synergistic manner these techniques can exponentially increase your sales.

Marketing your e-book outside of Kindle

One thing to keep in mind is that adding your ebook to additional marketplaces is not the same as marketing it on them. You will need to consider the extra workload and costs that will be incurred from your efforts to promote your book on these other websites.

If you do decide to market your e-book more widely than just Amazon you can use an aggregator such as Smashwords to distribute your book for you. If you publish your e-book with them they will then format and upload it to all of the other ebook venders for you such as iBook Barnes & Noble and all the rest without your having to lift a finger. For this service they will deduct 10% from your royalties for themselves so that you will be left with 60% rather than 70%. They do not take 10% of your Amazon royalties since they do not publish there. That market is still your responsibility. Since the e-book market outside of Amazon is about 35% of the world total and if your book is properly promoted on those other sites you might see an improvement in your royalty payments by as much as 30% The only way you will ever know for sure is to give it a try and see if it works for you.

12 KEYWORD SPREADSHEETS

I had to divide the spreadsheets into two or three segments to have any chance of fitting them onto a single page of the book. It makes no difference in what order you read them. The first one is for the heart failure book, which only has one section. The next page contains the two sections for the cancer cures book.

Each keyword phrase at the top of each column has a number after it, which indicates the number of pages of 16 books each that were returned by that keyword phrase when it was typed into the Kindle search bar. The column of numbers below the keyword phrases show the book's position for that keyword on that particular day. It indicates the position by book number so that if it is a "2" that would indicate that on that day it was the second book returned by the search, which would of course place it on the first page of results. "KW" indicates when keywords were added to the book's keyword list on its' detail page.

At the end of the last segment are lists for the number of reviews if any, the overall store rank, the category rank and any sales for that day. It is interesting how little the book positions change over time when the total number of books returned is 100 or less. When the number returned is greater than 100 the books position tends to fluctuate more. It is also apparent how few ebook versions of the "Cancer Cures book are being sold. Currently more copies of its' paperback version are selling than the ebook version. This is more than twice the normal ratio. The 30-day running total for both books combined is about $120 ($60 each).

This includes both CreateSpace and Kindle version royalties. About $30-$50 per month per book is what low interest ebooks produce in their Kindle version with about $20-$60 for the CreateSpace version. Large sales volume only happens when you write a book on a trending topic where the market is not saturated.

Very specialized books of this nature just do not sell very well and there is nothing that you can do to improve this other than doing what has already been recommended in preceding chapters. It is worth noting that these books are currently outselling most of the others of the same type and the ones that are ahead of them in sales have an emotional angle to exploit as well as being backed up by the considerable resources of a traditional publisher, which means that many of the buyers on kindle originally saw them in a real book store or in other advertisements and then decided to buy it cheaper on Kindle.

	Sept.	CHF2 Heart Failure38	Congestive Heart Failure17	Coronary Heart Disease28	Heart Health216	Heart Disease170	Heart Attack31	Reviews	O Rank	C Rank	Sales
65	Sept.										
66	1st	1	10	1	22	172	43	31	2	54k	11	2
67	2nd	1	10	1	15	160	48	20	1	60k	12	1
68	3rd	1	10	1	15	164	57	28	0	76k	13	1
69	4th	1	10	1	18	177	48	27	1	84k	12	1
70	5th	1	2	1	16	133	48	19	1	75k	10	1
71	6th	1	10	1	2	131	48	20	0	51k	9	1
72	7th	1	10	1	2	181	50	20	1	157k	32	1
73	8th	1	10	1	18	138	50	28	0	253k	74	0
74	9th	1	10	1	19	110	48	21	0	210k	65	0
75	10th	1	10	1	18	103	54	28	0	284k	70	2
76	11th	1	10	1	19	149	55	30	0	197k	53	0
77	12th	1	10	1	25	114	61	20	0	90k	18	1
78	13th	1	10	1	33	113	53	28	0	212k	59	0
79	14th	1	10	1	8	111	54	28	0	281k	78	0
80	15th	1	10	1	17	142	64	28	0	327k	98	1
81	16th	1	10	1	25	160	69	27	0	121k	29	0
82	17th	1	10	1	17	158	71	22	0	133k	30	1
83	18th	1	10	1	18	144	83	21	0	140k	45	0
84	19th	1	10	1	15	148	85	28	0	242k	57	1
85	25th	1	10	1	27	159	87	29	0	103k	17	1
86	28th	1	10	1	26	122	69	21	0	239k	56	1

	Breast Cancer cures9	Breast Cancer treatment9	Breast Cancer prevention9	Breast Cancer120	Colon Cancer18	Colorectal Cancer11	Leukemia34	Lung Cancer28	Prostate Cancer43	sales	Reviews	O Rank	C Rank	Keyword Version
1	4	56	33	170	17	9	35	41	79	0	0	643k	461	4 1st
2	4	48	27	172	13	11	41	39	77	0	0	662k	483	4 2nd
3	5	42	22	163	12	12	37	42	73	0	0	683k	507	4 3rd
4	2	36	17	165	17	8	41	44	81	3	1	83k	36 Alerrandre cover	4th
5	3	36	26	167	25	8	28	44	75	0	0	84k	34 Category Change 1	5th
6	7	47	19	159	22	9	31	37	72	26	1	100k	3 BB Promo .99	6th
7	12	52	24	153	28	16	33	36	69	16	1	10k	3 BB Promo .99	7th
8	3	42	18	73	8	17	31	37	71	8	0	19k	5 BB Promo .99	8th
9	9	42	43	63	8	15	32	43	56	6	1	18k	5 Hotzippy Promo .99 9th
10	9	37	25	63	17	15	7	36	56	3	0	32k	11 Hotzippy Promo .99 10th
11	9	37	26	56	25	15	9	36	56	1	1	47k	15 $2.99 11th
12	9	37	25	63	25	8	15	36	55	0	1	42k	14	4 12th
13	10	29	25	63	16	5	15	44	63	0	0	60k	22	4 13th
14	9	29	18	70	17	5	15	44	63	0	0	130k	50	4 14th
15	2	31	17	71	16	6	21	45	63	0	0	166k	73	4 15th
16	2	31	25	89	18	6	27	39	64	0	0	207k	102	4 16th
17	9	33	17	82	16	6	21	45	65	1	0	241k	112	4 17th
18	2	24	16	88	8	7	21	47	56	0	0	100k	38	4 18th
19	9	32	20	115	18	17	24	30	66	4	0	75k	26	4 24th
20	9	45	20	117	18	17	31	43	67	1	0	121k	47	4 25th
21		42	27	105	16	17	22	43	75	1	0	302k	168	4 28th

September	Cancer400	Cancer Cures39	Cancer Stories63	Natural Cancer Cures9	Natural Cancer Treatment99	Cancer Treatment6	Cancer Treatment99	Alternative Cancer Treatment17	Alternative Cancer Treatment	Cancer Prevention5	Cancer Prevention38	Breast Cancer cures9
1st	498	4		10	130	11	46	14	10	31	4	
2nd	558	11		11		10	43	11	5	28	4	
3rd	572	8		10		11	35	13	4	33	5	
4th	563	4		10		11	22	14	3	31	2	
5th	432	6		12		13	32	16	7	25	3	
6th	349	12		14		16	28	16	9	35	3	
7th	338	16		13		14	24	18	5	27	7	
8th	89	10		3		8	23	18	11	29	12	
9th	69	9	27	2		12	21	7	10	29	3	
10th	75	3	30	9		4	29	14	10	21	9	
11th	69	3	23	1		12	29	6	10	29	9	
12th	71	3	31	2		4	21	5	9	28	9	
13th	93	3	32	2		11	26	5	9	31	10	
14th	94	3	33	9		11	20	13	2	22	9	
15th	112	3	32	2		11	20	13	2	22	9	
16th	145	3	41	2		11	28	6	10	30	2	
17th	225	3	35	2		11	28	6	10	23	9	
18th	202	3	35	10		11	21	7		21	9	
19th	212	11	24	10		11	30	30		22	2	
24th	222	3	23	10		11	23	15		31	9	
25th	221	11	35	10		11	23	15		23	9	

13 CONCLUSIONS

Here are the monthly download stats for both the Kindle and CreateSpace versions of the two books. The first column shows sales prior to making our changes. The second column shows the improvement in sales after all of the changes were made. The ebook sales have doubled but the paperback sales have tripled. Normally paperback sales should be about 50% of eBook sales. The greater sales for these two books are probably the result of older people, who need this type of information, preferring a physical rather than electronic version of the books.

If nothing else this proves that it is absolutely necessary to publish your book in both Kindle and CreateSpace versions. Also a paperback book is held to a higher standard than an eBook so attention to detail is even more important for generating sales.

Book Name	Before	After Changes
Cancer Cures eBook	6 per month	11 per month
Heart Failure eBook	11 per month	22 per month
Cancer Cures CS	5 per month	19 per month
Heart Failure CS	7 per month	20 per month

The only three things that make a long-term difference in sales are:

The Subject mater's popularity.

Your particular book's popularity in relationship to others in its' category.

Your book's visibility within the system

As we saw in the "Title Creation" chapter optimization of the books title is the most effective promotional tool that you have. I am repeating those two pages from that chapter here to make sure that everyone is aware of the importance of this for maximizing sales.

We changed the title of Ray's heart book from "Congestive Heart Failure Recovery" with the subtitle "From Complete Failure to Complete Recovery" to "Heart Failure" with the subtitle "From complete Heart Failure to Heart Health"

The number after each search phrase is the total number of pages of 16 books each returned by the search. The columns of numbers in the other two columns indicate the position of the book in the search results.

Search Phrase	Before Change	After Change
CHF2	1	1
Heart Failure38	10	1
Congestive Heart Failure17	1	1
Heart Health216	122	13
Heart Disease170	69	27
Heart Attack31	21	5

We changed the title of his cancer book from "Cancer Cures" with the subtitle "A Synergistic Approach to Cancer Prevention and Treatment" to "Cancer" with the subtitle "Cures, a Synergistic Approach to Cancer Prevention and Treatment"

Search Phrase	Before Change	After Change
Cancer400	221	21
Cancer Cures39	11	4
Cancer Stories63	35	4
Natural Cancer Cures9	10	5
Natural Cancer Treatment6	11	9
Cancer Treatment99	23	10
Alternative Cancer Treatment	15	2
Alternative Cancer Prevention5	4	9
Cancer Prevention38	23	6
Breast Cancer Cures9	9	10
Breast Cancer Prevention9	27	12
Breast Cancer Treatment9	42	3
Breast Cancer120	105	29
Colon Cancer18	16	11
Colorectal Cancer11	17	1
Lung Cancer28	43	13
Prostate Cancer43	75	13
Leukemia34	22	37

I would call that a significant change for the better! I am not certain as to why there is such a difference between the titles "Cancer Cures" and "Cancer". Obviously much experimentation is needed whenever you create a title so that you discover anomalies such as this. Even the search phrase "cancer cures" gives better results when the title is just "Cancer" than when it is "Cancer Cures". That is not logical! This only seems to work when the most common search phrase used is a single word such as "cancer".

If searching for books on "heart failure" titling them just "heart" would not work. However naming a book "Knitting" or "Baking" then a subtitle that expands upon it probably would be very effective because that is what a potential customer would be most likely to enter as a search phrase. This is why you need to publish your Kindle version before your CreateSpace version so that you can perfect the title before committing yourself to a title in CreateSpace that can never be changed.

It may be because everyone who searches for books on cancer only enters "Cancer" instead of more detailed search phrases so the search engine has decided that that is the one to treat preferentially. This shows that when we ourselves are searching for books on a subject we need to be very diligent about using a variety of detailed search phrases to avoid missing appropriate books that will not be found with more general one-word search phrases.

When your title is only one word you need to make sure that other potential search words are located elsewhere in the subtitle, keywords and description. I will continue my research in this area and upload that new information in the first revision of this book in about two months, which you can then download free of charge because you have already purchased it. I will also be including the statistics for this book and others that I research. Check back every couple of months for higher revision numbers than what you currently have.

After uploading this book to KDP and doing the first round of testing I found that none of the obvious search phrases found it so I changed the title from "Reality based Kindle Publishing" to just "Kindle Publishing". Immediately after the change was reviewed and approved the search phrase "kindle publishing" returned it in the number three position on the first page of results out of 400 pages of books. I will continue optimizing all of its' parameters and include that information in the first revision to this book in a couple of months.

Sales promotions

Below are screenshots of the sales for both books for 90-day periods. It is obvious that after any book promotion the book will return to its' previous level of sales. Promotions are only effective for generating reviews and temporary increases in sales ranking within the Amazon environment. You will probably generate more sales by listing your book on the various book information depositories such as goodreads.com. These are free and will let potential buyers for books such as yours know that yours exists should they do a search of their database.

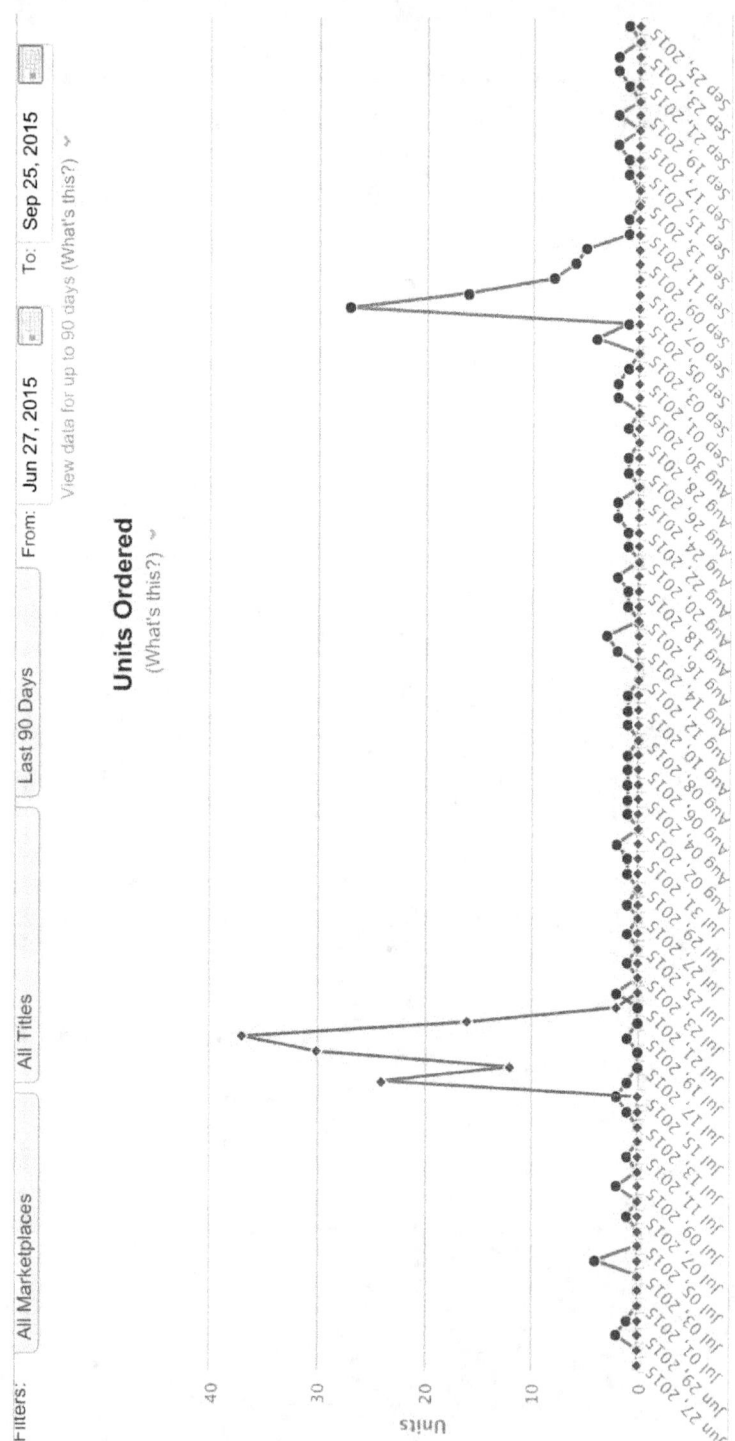

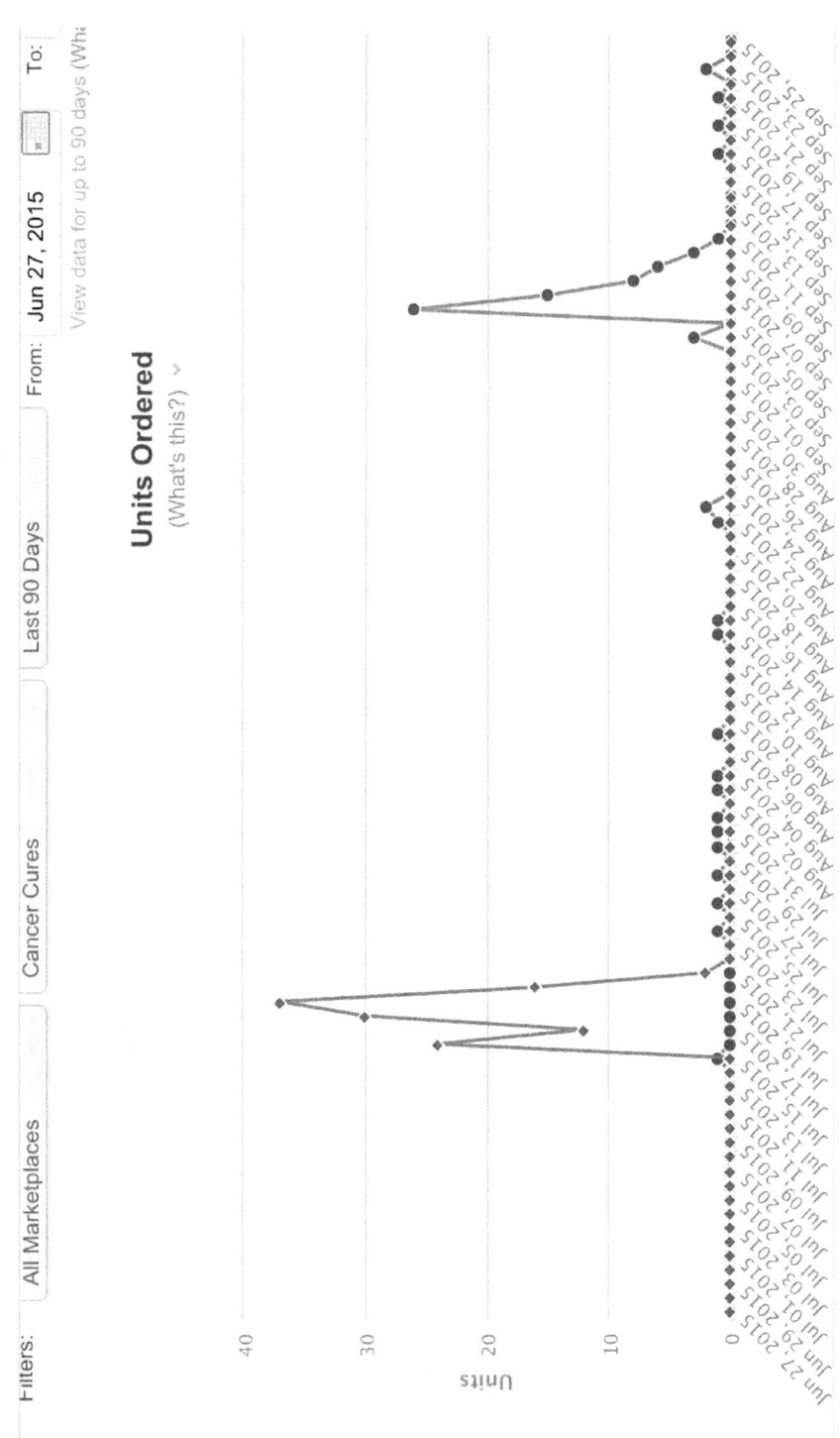

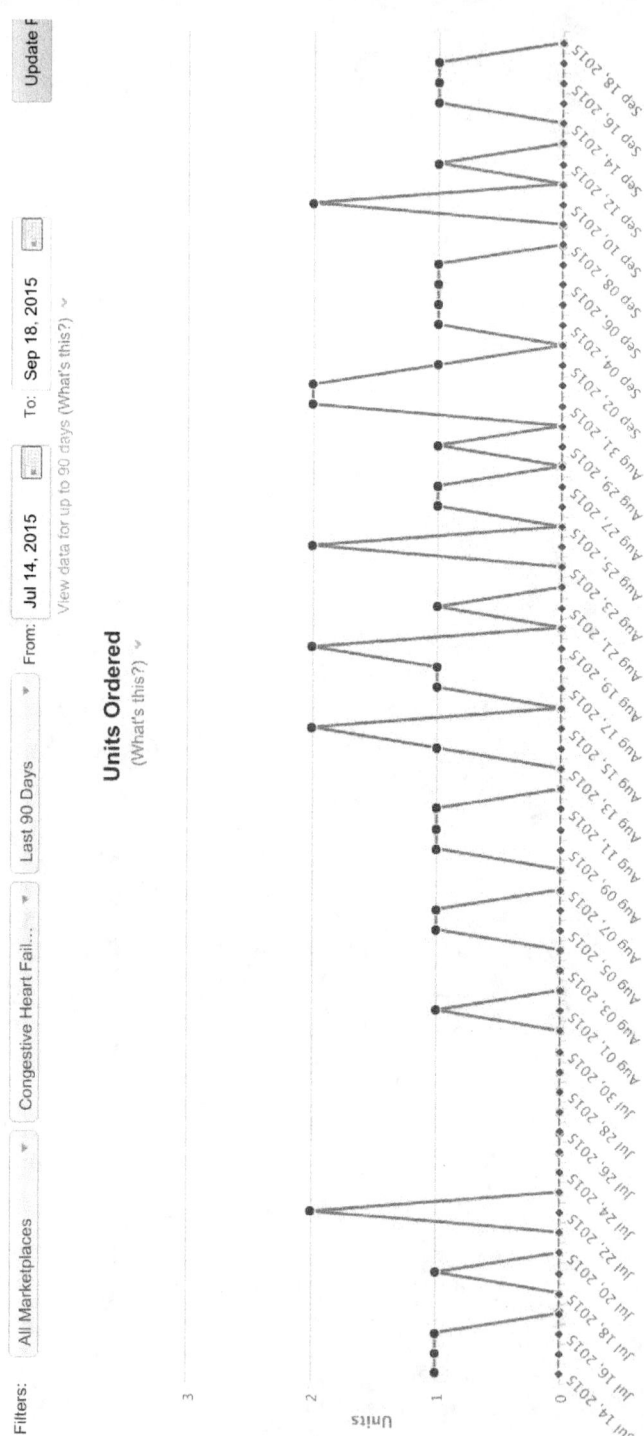

www.ingramcontent.com/pod-product-compliance
Lightning Source LLC
Chambersburg PA
CBHW071405280526
45787CB00001B/446